RmEF
moi

Best wishes,

Jim Zumbo

To Heck With
Moose Hunting

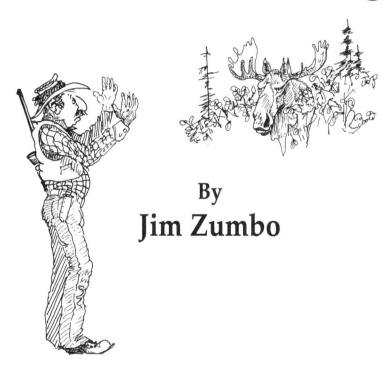

By
Jim Zumbo

All photos by the author unless otherwise noted.

Illustrations by Boots Reynolds

Dedication

To my wife, Madonna,
my favorite hunting companion.

Copyright © 1996 by Jim Zumbo

ISBN: 0-9624025-5-9

Published by:
Jim Zumbo
Wapiti Valley Publishing Company
P.O. Box 2390
Cody, Wyoming 82414
(307) 587-5486

TABLE OF CONTENTS

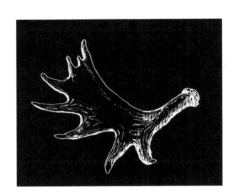

I TRIED TO SHOOT COLORADO'S BIGGEST MOOSE

"What's that?" my wife said as I drove slowly along the forest road.

"What's what?" I asked.

"A big black shape, I think," she responded. "It looked like a moose, but it's probably just a shadow."

For the hundredth time that day I stopped the pickup truck and backed up to look at a dark suspect form in the woods. So far we had spotted all sorts of black stumps, clumps of brush, logs, and other assorted forest objects that might be taken for a moose. I had no reason to believe that she'd seen a real, honest to God moose. Neither did Larry Weishuhn, a well known outdoor writer from Texas who was riding along with us. Like me, Larry had also drawn a Colorado moose tag, but his was in a unit adjacent to mine.

Our plan for the day was to scout my area from the road, and later we'd drive over to his unit. The season opened in the morning for both units. Looking for moose from the road might seem to be a lazy man's way of scouting, but I never knock a system that works. Moose aren't exactly the brightest critters on the planet, and a good share of them are quite willing to graze along roads and tolerate the presence of people. Since we had no horses, I was hoping to drop my prize so we could transport it to the truck easily. As they often say, "The best moose is the one that falls closest to the road." Heck, I was hoping to shoot one about a yard away from the road.

I backed up and we all looked in the direction where Madonna had seen a dark form. "My God, it is a moose." Larry said excitedly, "What a bull!" It was indeed. I couldn't believe it. Walking in the willows next to the road was a grand bull, in fact the biggest bull moose I'd ever seen in the Rockies. He appeared to have a dozen points on each side, with tall broad palms. This was definitely the boss moose of the woods.

Big problem. How many other hunters with a moose tag had spotted this bull? He seemed quite relaxed and unafraid, even though we were sitting in my pick-up just 75 yards away.

Concerned that other hunters might come along the road, we took one last look before I drove away. No sense calling attention to this monster moose, even though I could have looked at him for hours. Madonna was making modest little statements to suggest that it was just a lucky find, but I knew better. She has great game eyes, often spotting animals long before the rest of us in the party.

Larry and I were beside ourselves. This was a serious moose, one that deserved my exclusive attention when the season opened in the morning. Interestingly enough, Larry had just returned from a moose hunt in Maine where he'd taken a fine bull. Maine has plenty of big moose, but he admitted he hadn't seen anything even close to this colossal Colorado bull. What's more, the moose we were to hunt is the Shiras subspecies that inhabits the Rocky Mountains. They are the smallest of the three subspecies, including the animals in Maine which are actually Canada moose, the second biggest. The largest is the Alaska-Yukon moose. In all my years of hunting moose in North America, the bull that Madonna had spotted was right at the top of the list.

Drawing the Colorado moose tag was cause for great celebration. Odds were tough, and I was a mighty happy camper when I got the news because there were only a few non-resident moose tags issued in the state. I owed my good luck to my pal, George Taulman, of Taos, New Mexico, who runs a licensing service in the West. George keeps track of all the odds for western big game, and for a small fee, acts as your agent and applies you for whatever tags interest you. Madonna also drew a moose tag through George's licensing system the year before — a Utah moose — but that's another chapter. (If you're interested in George's program, call him at 1-800-845-9929).

Given the fact that I literally hunt about 130 days a year, you might say that some of the thrill of anticipating the hunt has been a bit diminished. That's not to say, however, that I don't get excited — it's just that I don't lose quite as much sleep as I used to. I knew as soon as we drove away from that bull however, that this would be one of those rare sleepless nights. As it turned out, I was right.

As I mentioned, I didn't want to observe the bull any longer than usual, because I was afraid that another moose hunter would come along and see the bull. As it was, there was a hunting camp about 60 yards below the little willow bottom that the bull was walking in, and another camp about 100 yards above it. The distance between the camps was 400 yards, and I had no idea what those hunters were hunting. Deer and elk season also opened in the morning. Did any of those hunters have moose tags, and had this bull been hanging around next to the road where he'd been easily spotted? Those were some of the questions that were to keep me awake that night. It just seemed too easy. The moose was too bold, too many people were around.

After driving over to Larry's unit and watching two bulls, one of them a youngster and the other a very nice 40-incher, we drove back to my Jayco camp trailer that was parked about 30 miles away in another part of the national forest. I had parked the camp trailer there the week before while on my way to an elk hunt in New Mexico. Though I'd done just a minimal amount of scouting when I dropped off the camper, I'd talked to enough people who had all sorts of advice. My informants ranged from hunting friends who knew the area, sporting goods store employees, game wardens, and wildlife biologists. Every one of them said I shouldn't have a problem finding a bull moose, even though the season was only five days long.

What made this hunt special was my involvement with the Colorado moose success story that started in 1979 and 1980. Utah and Wyoming wildlife personnel captured some of their moose and released them in Colorado, where moose had never lived before. I covered those stories intensely, and closely watched the growing and thriving moose herd in Colorado. Of course, I had no clue that one day I'd draw a moose tag.

Joining us on the hunt were two of George's employees who would videotape the hunt. Neither of the men, Pockets (George named him that because he couldn't keep his hands out of his pockets) nor Jerry were professional photographers, especially with the large and very expensive cameras that they would be using. To learn how to operate the cameras, some of the photographers who worked full time for Bill Jordan's company, Spartan-Realtree, put on a training session and taught several of George's men how to run the complicated cameras.

Jerry and Pockets had a tent set up, along with a heater and cots. Larry would bunk with them; Madonna and I and our black Labrador dog, Shike, would stay in our camp trailer. Shike would be allowed to ride in the back seat of the pickup, but he wouldn't be doing any running at large. If we parked the truck and went for an extended walk, Shike would snooze in the cab of the pickup while we were gone.

I had volunteered to do the cooking for the whole crew and wasted no time by thawing a big container of the elk stew that I had previously cooked for the first night's dinner. I had pre-cooked and frozen most of the meals to save time, assuming we'd be getting back to camp well after dark each night.

I was ready to go when the alarm went off at 4:00 am; in fact I was ready to go at midnight. Sleep was not part of the plan that evening.

Madonna, Pockets, and I left camp well before sunup. Obviously, I'd begin the search where we'd seen the giant bull. There were no other options, not with a bruiser moose like we'd seen running around.

As I approached the spot, I half expected to see a pickup or two along the road where we'd spotted the moose. I was relieved to learn that I was wrong. The hunting camps above and below the willow bottom were active, though. Lanterns illuminated the tents and we could see people moving around. Again — the big question — had any of them seen the bull, and did anyone have a moose tag?

*This big Shiras moose may be the smallest subspecies,
but it's still a huge animal.*

As soon as it was light enough to see, we strained our eyes to see into the willows. Anticipation and excitement were sky high, but no moose appeared. Once we established that the bull wasn't present, we headed out across the road from where we'd seen the moose. This was a clear cut area, with a creek lined with willows running along the perimeter. Maybe our boss of the mountain would be somewhere close by.

About 20 minutes after hiking through the area, Madonna spotted a moose at the edge of the timber. It turned out to be a modest 30-inch bull, a moose that would have probably been welcome by most other hunters, but certainly wasn't in the same stature of the boss bull. I opted to pass.

We continued walking toward a small rise, and looked down into a lovely basin blanketed with quaking aspen trees. We followed an old road down and about half way I decided to try calling a moose. Using just my mouth without an artificial moose call, I gave a few grunts and immediately heard a response from the willows. A few minutes later, after calling back and forth, a bull showed up. Again it was a modest bull, with 20 to 25-inch antlers, but still not good enough for opening day.

The bull approached fairly closely, within about 30 feet, before he realized we weren't part of his own kind. He turned and left in a hurry, and that's about when we saw several elk running through the area just below us, probably spooked by some other hunters. We'd heard a shot or two from that direction a few minutes earlier.

I might mention that our photographer was so impressed at the sight of that bull moose that he forgot to turn the camera on. I had to remind him, and when he realized the mistake, he quickly started shooting film, but it was almost too late.

We continued hunting up and down the road in the general area where we'd seen the big bull. We hiked up trails, through timbered areas and in willow thickets, hoping to catch sight of him. But no dice. Mr. Big wasn't showing.

Later on we drove down the road to an area we hadn't been to before, and saw a very big willow bottom that was probably 20 acres in size. In the bottom we saw a cow and a calf moose, and I was convinced that this was the place that a big bull might hang out, hopefully the big boy that we were after. Since the rut was on, I figured he'd be traveling, looking for cows, and this was a likely spot. This was one of the nicest moose habitat areas I'd seen on the entire forest, and I had a hunch it would pay off for us later on in the hunt.

We didn't see much the rest of the day, although we found out that the shots we'd heard that morning were taken by a young boy who was fourteen years old. He had killed a very nice 5 x 5 bull elk. The youngster and his family were from the Lake states, and this was the boy's first hunt. We went by his camp and congratulated him, and of course we asked hunters there, as well as every place else we went, if they had seen any bull moose.

At that point the answer was basically negative, because it was opening day and hunters hadn't gotten around very much yet. We made the long drive home across the forest to our camper and arrived well after sundown. The drive itself from where we saw the big bull, back to camp was probably 20 miles, and took a good hour and a half across the forest roads. But, I wasn't about to try the area near camp when I knew the big bull might show up any time in the original area where we had spotted him. I learned that there were a number of moose literally within a few hundred yards of where we were camped, but I still felt there was no choice. It was either the big bull or nothing.

While scouting before the season we ran into a couple of cowboys who were herding some cattle off the mountain. They told us they'd seen a pretty big bull somewhere close to timberline. But that was before we'd spotted the monster moose, and I still wasn't interested in varying my plan to try for the big boy.

The next morning we drove back to our hunting area, and continued to look for the moose. To my dismay, nothing showed up. A little while later, we went to the big willow bottom, and sure enough, there were three bulls in it. None were really interesting, though one of the bulls would have tempted me had I not seen the big one. That particular bull in the willow bottom had a 40 inch spread, but the shovels were narrow and he only had four or five points on each palm.

I decided to hold off and take this moose on the last day of the hunt, provided he was still there and I didn't get the big one. At that time I still didn't know how many other moose hunters were in the area, but from figuring out how many permits there were, I deducted that I was probably the only hunter with a bull license in that part of the unit. We ran into two other hunters at the willow bottom who had a cow tag. And even though there was a cow out there, the hunter with the tag was reluctant to try for her because the bottom was extremely marshy and almost to the point of being quicksand. It was virtually impossible to get through it, and they weren't about to shoot a cow and not have a way to retrieve her. Good thinking, I thought.

Later that afternoon we ran into some hunters who had seen a big bull moose in an area we hadn't hunted yet. I was vaguely familiar with the place, having considered going in there one day. We headed over and hiked in to where the hunter claimed to have spotted the moose.

We walked probably two miles. When we stopped to take a

break, I started making moose sounds and suddenly I got a response. Another moose was answering. Out he came, a small bull with a 25 inch-wide rack, looking for the source of the grunts. He seemed to look at us and paid little attention, but kept casually walking within about 50 yards. Finally he disappeared, but again I had to remind Pockets, the cameraman, to shoot some footage because he was so mesmerized by the moose's presence.

As it was turning out, many of the elk and deer hunters were starting to see some moose and were quite willing to share information with us on what they'd seen. It was difficult to get them to describe how big the moose was. For example, one hunter said he'd seen a big moose. I asked him how big. He said, "It was really big." Then I asked about how wide his rack was, and what it looked like. The hunter again replied, "It was really big, it probably weighed 2,000 pounds." He couldn't quite define the size of the rack, and I was fairly sure that this hunter, like most others, was so impressed with the size of the moose that any bull moose was a big bull moose. Of course, none of them had seen the giant bull (or so I assumed), and couldn't know what I was looking for.

On day three we headed back out. This time, we crossed the forest over a different route, topping out at a pass that at first I had declined to try because we had word that it was pretty slick and nasty. However, we found it fair going, and got into some brand new country up above timberline. We saw some moose tracks in the snow, but again I wasn't quite willing to spend a whole lot of time away from the area where we had seen Mister Big. I always had the nagging feeling that he would show up at any moment and we'd be a long way away. Nonetheless, I forced myself to look elsewhere because I was starting to get the feeling that that particular bull might have left the area. In fact, when we'd seen him, he seemed to be walking with purpose. He wasn't browsing as he walked, but was striding slowly up the willow bottom as if he had an objective in mind. Since the rut was on, I was fearful that he might have left the country and we'd never see him again.

A break came, or so we thought, when a hunter told us that he'd seen the giant bull while he was making a nature call behind his camp. Still, I wasn't positive that this was the huge bull. The hunter really couldn't describe the bull, again saying that it was just a great big bull. He couldn't tell me how wide the antlers might have been, or how many points on each side. The 40-inch bull I'd passed up in the willow bottom would be a great big bull to most anyone. Except to me, Madonna, and Larry. We knew better.

On day four I was starting to get more than a little nervous. I had almost convinced myself that the big moose had left the area. That morning, while driving down the road, a bull with a two-foot spread crossed in front of us and stood alongside the road. He would have been a tempting target at any other time, especially where he was standing, because I could easily have backed the truck up to him and loaded him into it. But still, I was looking for the big boy, though I'll admit the fat bull glaring at us looked awfully good. I could just picture all the steaks, roasts, ribs, and burger standing there in that big, black package. But I drove away, shaking my head.

The old faithful willow bottom was again producing moose, this time a bull and a cow. They didn't seem to be disturbed. The cow hunter had gone elsewhere and had given up on the willow swamp. As he had told us at his camp, he hunted on another part of the forest and indeed got his cow. That was good news, since that left no other moose hunters at all in the part of the unit that I was hunting.

I made up my mind that on the last day I'd take any bull. Chances of ever drawing a moose tag again in Colorado were slim to none. Besides, my wife's parents had purchased a brand new freezer, exclusively to fill it with moose meat. I had convinced them that the moose hunt was almost always a 100 percent successful affair and practically guaranteed them that we'd come home with a moose. The pressure was on, and I really wasn't worried about finding a bull the last day. After all, hadn't I seen at least one bull so far every day of the hunt?

Larry had taken a nice bull with a three foot spread. He shot the bull with a handgun in his unit which bordered mine. He was able to drive fairly close to the moose and had the bull hanging in camp the evening of the fourth day.

The last day, I was ready for any moose. As I said, I was convinced at this point that the big bull was probably gone because certainly someone would have seen it and would have been impressed enough that they would have been able to describe his enormous antlers. That had not been the case so far.

As luck would have it (bad luck), we saw no moose that morning, not even in the willow bottom. I wasn't sure what to do, but I had two plans. One was to ease around the forest that surrounded the willow bottom and look for a moose in the woods there. Certainly an animal had to be close to that willow swamp. It was thick enough that there were places we couldn't see animals, in fact, some of the moose that we'd spotted were seen only after we'd been there 15 or 20 minutes, looking intently through binoculars and a spotting scope. The cover in the swamp was extremely heavy in places.

Madonna and I and the photographer eased through the forest and found incredible trails. Fresh moose sign was everywhere, but no moose. We walked completely around the perimeter of the big willow bottom, and looked into the brush from every angle we could. I concluded that there wasn't a moose anywhere near the area that day.

I couldn't believe it! The old faithful willow bottom had been a moose Mecca. Wouldn't you know, that on this last day of the season, all the moose would be gone? Was I not living right, or what?

We headed for the place that I had called in the moose on the second day because other hunters had claimed they had seen moose there fairly consistently. This was going to be the place for our last stand.

Before leaving the truck, we let Shike out for a quick walk. Suddenly he bolted, ran across the road and up into the hillside. Madonna followed, hoping to catch up with him. I would have been more amused, because the dog typically didn't disobey, but there were only a few more hours of moose season left. What I didn't need was my dog lost in the woods, with a panicky wife trying to find her baby.

Suddenly I heard Madonna yelling and I knew something was wrong. I couldn't see what was happening because all the action was about 50 yards away. I ran as fast as I could up the hill and heard Madonna saying something to the effect that a porcupine was involved with our beloved pooch. Having been the owner of several dogs, and having been in porcupine country before, I knew exactly what had happened. There was no doubt in my mind that Shike had gotten into it with a porky.

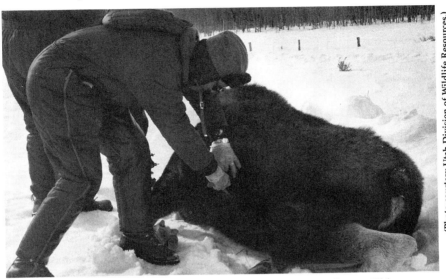

Utah biologists work on a tranquilized moose that will be relocated to Colorado.

I was right. Catching up to Shike, I pulled him away from the tree that held an upset porcupine. Shike, as I fully expected, had a face full of quills. I managed to sit and calm him down, and performed a quill retraction project with the pliers that I had in my daypack. He was a lucky Labrador, since he only had 30 or 40 quills in his face. I've seen cases where dogs had picked up several hundred, with some in their tongues. Ouch!

With the operation on Shike over with, we made our last ditch effort and hiked down into the area where we hoped to see a bull. Many things went through my mind as we sat there. It had been an interesting hunt for the huge bull, and I'll admit there was plenty of anticipation every day. But, now it was time to conclude the hunt. I wondered how it would feel to go home that night if we didn't see a moose, knowing that I would probably be the only unsuccessful nonresident that ever hunted the state of Colorado for moose. Actually, that didn't bother me very much because it had been a good hunt and I had been pursuing a particular animal that was undoubtedly one of the biggest moose in all of the Rocky Mountains. Besides, I had plenty of opportunities. Had I wanted a bull, it was there for the taking.

With sundown that night came the stark reality that this hunt was history. We headed back to camp almost laughing, because here we were with a tag that most other hunters could easily fill, yet we were going home empty. Madonna agreed that she, and not me, would tell her parents that there was no moose for their new freezer. After all, wasn't it her fault that I didn't get a moose? If she hadn't spotted El Brute, we'd have been home long ago.

As I learned, the five day hunt in Colorado didn't allow much time if one was looking for a really big moose. To my knowledge, every other western state offers at least a 30-day season; some much longer. I can't really fault Colorado, however. As I just mentioned, I had plenty of chances.

I didn't say to heck with moose hunting however, although I figured I was done forever in Colorado because it was a once in a lifetime hunt. Imagine my pleasant surprise later, when I learned that the once in a lifetime rule applied only if you had killed a moose. I'd actually get another chance if, of course, I could draw another tag.

There's an interesting sequel to this story, although interesting may not be the right word. Call it incredible. Several months after the moose hunt I received a note from a Colorado hunter with a newspaper clipping about a moose he'd taken in the unit adjacent to mine. The newspaper clipping showed a huge, huge moose. I was almost positive this was the exact same bull that I was hunting. This bull, after being scored, was the biggest moose ever to come from the state of Colorado, and the third biggest Shiras moose in the world. The bull was killed about four miles from where we'd seen him the day before the season. That's just a casual stroll for a bull looking for cows.

Somehow that news made me feel better, if indeed it was the same bull (the photos convinced me it was). Knowing that I had been chasing the biggest moose in Colorado made my actions all the more justified.

HURRY UP
AND SHOOT THE WOLF

I've always had a fascination for the north. So it was with a great deal of excitement when I booked a moose and caribou trip with the Collingwood brothers who were based out of Smithers, British Columbia.

Ray and Reggie Collingwood are widely known outfitters who hunt the huge Spatsizi Provincial Park in northern B.C. They basically have exclusive rights for Spatsizi and they specialize in moose, stone sheep, caribou, as well as mountain goats, grizzlies, black bears, and wolves. These were the outfitters, as you may recall, that were involved in a confrontation with members of Greenpeace many years ago. The Greenpeace people had been harassing the Collingwoods and their clients for two years and subsequently the whole matter ended up in a fist fight. Let's just say that the Collingwoods and their guides won big time. Litigation afterward was on the side of Collingwoods; Greenpeace lost. Maybe there's a little justice on this planet after all.

I'd met the Collingwoods at sports shows before and always enjoyed their company. They're honest, hard-working outfitters who know what they're doing in that vast, remote piece of landscape.

I flew into Smithers the day before my departure to hunting camp and visited with Ray Collingwood over dinner. Ray is the business brains of the company and is also an outstanding bush pilot. He does a great deal of the flying while Reggie does most of the guiding and manages the backcountry camps.

Actually, this was my second trip to the Spatsizi area. A few years before, I was there in the summer on a fishing trip. That particular trip was with a company called Love Brothers and Lee who are legendary in that part of the world. It was in the same general area where the Collingwoods hunt.

This was one of the cabins used by hunters in the Collingwood camp.

When I left from that fishing trip, the fist-fight broke out a couple days later during the Collingwood hunt. I knew it was going to happen, because these people had been harassing Collingwoods for two years and something was about to go haywire. You don't mix up a bunch of flower children with backcountry guides who have vastly differing ideologies and come up with harp music.

As it turned out, it all ended up in favor of the Collingwoods. The people from Greenpeace said to heck with harassing those boys forevermore.

The next morning I flew from Smithers to Spatsizi in a small plane. As often happens in the north, bad weather was forecast, and we had a hurried trip. Flying in and out of heavy, gray clouds, the pilot did a nice job and made a fine landing at base camp. The pilot wasted no time getting back out of there, since the ceiling was rapidly dropping.

After meeting the camp personnel, I was shown to a comfortable log cabin where I'd stay for a couple days. The idea was to hunt moose out of base camp and then take horses to the Ross River, a well-known area in that region that has always held plenty of caribou and grizzlies.

The plan didn't quite work out that way. While in camp I looked off to the north with my spotting scope, just getting a feel for the country, and I saw a bull moose. I told Reggie about my discovery, and he looked at the moose.

"Are you ready to go moose hunting?" Reggie asked.

"Do fish swim?" I responded. (Reggie didn't know me very well, I'm always ready to hunt.)

My gear was hardly unpacked, but we hurriedly saddled up a couple horses along with a couple pack horses and headed for the moose.

Now then, it's one thing to spot an animal up on a mountainside and quite another to get to it. Although this moose appeared to be less than a mile away, it took three hours to get to that area--three hours of rough riding through some dense vegetation with few or no trails.

Upon approaching the area where we'd seen the moose, we tied up the horses and eased in through the brush. Soon afterward we heard antlers crashing against each other, and I knew a pair of bulls were sparring off somewhere below us. We slipped up close and got there just in time to see one of the bulls trotting away.

"Is he a good one?" I asked.

"Not a giant, but not bad. It's up to you," Reggie responded.

I thought about my priorities. Caribou were foremost, and we had only another day here which was the best moose area. Besides, other hunters would be joining us for the horseback ride to the Ross River.

One shot from my .30/06 put the moose down handily. Now came the work. As they say, the fun of a moose hunt is over when you press the trigger.

It turned out to be a nice moose, nothing spectacular, but nonetheless I was pleased with the animal. The bull had a 45-inch wide rack. Good enough. With the moose out of the way, I could now concentrate on a caribou. It was going to be a long, rough ride from base camp to get to where we were going to camp for caribou up the Ross River.

We dressed the moose, boned the meat, packed it on the horses and made it back to camp just before dark. Some of the meat would go to local Indians, but I wanted to take as much home as possible, given the weight limitations of the airplane that would fly me out. I'm totally enamored with moose meat, believing it to rank right at the top of all the big game animals I've sampled in North America, which includes most of them.

That evening, I met another hunter and his son who were destined to become lifelong friends. Lou Elorza, a veterinarian from British Columbia, was in camp to hunt with his son Ronnie. Although I actually didn't hunt with Lou, we made our acquaintance in camp and I was to see a great deal more of him and his lovely family in the future. Today we are still good friends. Lou was originally from Reno, Nevada, married a gal from South Dakota, and moved to British Columbia where he is reputed to have the largest veterinary territory in all of Canada.

Also in camp were Mike and Susan Golightly from Flagstaff, Arizona. Susan was along as an observer, and Mike was after a big caribou. I might add that the Spatsizi area is home to some of the biggest mountain caribou in Canada. The mountain caribou is one of five subspecies which live in North America (six subspecies if you count the Peary caribou that is recognized only by the Safari Club but not by the Boone and Crockett Club).

The next morning, Susan, Mike, Reggie, me, and another guide whose name escapes me, mounted our horses and headed for the Ross River. All in all, there were five of us with four pack horses carrying food and supplies. Hopefully the horses would be carrying caribou racks and meat back out as well.

Jim Zumbo with British Columbia bull that he spotted from camp.

The journey to camp was a long one, often following river courses and drainages. At one point, Reggie announced that a bear was off to our left. I stood up in the stirrups, and sure enough I saw a bear, not a grizzly that frequents this country, but a black bear, a very, very large black bear. Reggie said the bear was feeding on a moose gut pile from an earlier hunt the previous week.

We got off our horses and slipped up close to the bear where we could get a better look at it. Never in my life have I seen a bigger black bear. This animal was huge, with a broad enormous head. We figured it would weigh 600 pounds or more. That's the good news. The bad news was that I didn't have a bear tag, neither did anyone else in our party. Dumb move on my part. Real dumb.

While buying my licenses in town before the hunt, I asked Ray if I should bother buying a bear and wolf tag along with the caribou and moose tags. Ray said black bears were very uncommon in the area, so I probably shouldn't waste my money, but it was always possible for a wolf to show up, although the odds of that happening were highly unlikely. Unfortunately for me, I opted to save $50 and didn't buy the black bear tag but I did buy a wolf tag, which also cost $50. I wish I could have known that there was the option of seeing that black bear when I had the chance of buying the tag. Oh well, you know what we say about hindsight...

However, you can bet that right there and then, while looking at the giant black bear, I said to heck with declining to buy tags for any legal animals on my hunts, no matter how remote the chances of seeing one might be.

We watched the bear for a while longer, and he wasn't about to leave his prize. He'd stand up on his hind feet, glare at us, roar, pop his teeth and otherwise act in a menacing fashion. Of course, we didn't get very close but maintained a safe distance. When we finally rode away, I looked back at the bear once again. I just couldn't get over how big he was.

About an hour later, when we were heading through a swamp, Reggie warned us that there were some deep mucky holes in the swamp and to try to keep the horses lined up behind each other. He'd lead the way and hopefully we'd miss the holes.

That was not to be. Wouldn't you know that every horse made it through that swamp except mine? Captain, my horse, managed to step into a bottomless piece of muck and immediately went down to his chin. I bailed off, jumping out of the stirrups at the last second and rolled off to the side. Luckily I landed on a little hummock of brush and didn't quite become encompassed by the oozing black muck, although I did manage to receive a generous coating of the smelly stuff. The laugh was on me, but everyone else sat on their horses, not knowing whether to smile, act serious, or offer condolences. I found it to be a bit humorous however, and mentioned something about my horse's lack of brains. My companions had a good laugh, and we rode away, with me muttering something about Murphy's Law.

We arrived at camp a couple hours after the incident in the swamp. Actually, camp was simply a big tarp lashed over some poles. All of us would share the large shelter. We were in very active grizzly country, so it was understandable why Susan wasn't really very excited about taking a walk in the dark woods to answer a nature call. Mike accompanied her, and of course, carried his rifle. Truth be known, I wasn't all that enthused about a nighttime stroll, either. I'd interviewed too many victims of grizzly attacks for my magazine articles. Yes, the .30/06 went where I went.

Interestingly enough, we had yet to run into a grizzly so far on the trip, though Lou Elorza and Ronnie had a big bear follow them into camp as they were returning from the day's hunt.

The next morning, we were preparing to head to the plateaus where the caribou lived. This was a unique area. We were actually camped along the Ross River, but the caribou were high up on plateaus that had vast expanses of ice fields. I was just about to untie the halter rope of my horse when Reggie suddenly shouted, "Get a gun. Hurry up, somebody get a gun." I had no idea what Reggie was talking about and I couldn't see him because he was over on the other side of the shelter. I could tell however, that the excitement in Reggie's voice was cause for urgency. I yanked my rifle from the scabbard and again heard Reggie say, "Hurry! Hurry, get a gun."

"What is it?" I yelled at Reggie as I chambered a live round.

"A wolf, a wolf! Hurry and shoot it," Reggie shouted.

Running around to where Reggie was, I saw him looking off to the side of camp. There, sitting on the ground looking at us intently, was a large wolf. I couldn't believe it. This was a wolf, an animal that is so rarely seen in the north country. A real live wolf! It looked to me like a big German shepard, but I knew that couldn't be possible. But what was a wolf doing, sitting there, staring at us no less than 60 feet from our tent?

Realizing that I had a wolf tag in my pocket and here sat a

wolf, I did the most natural thing. I centered the wolf squarely in the scope and pressed the trigger. I was now the owner of a wolf.

We rushed over to examine it and found it to be a male, not quite fully grown, but close enough. Interestingly, Mike's guide was born and raised in the northern part of B.C., and he said that he'd never seen a wolf. Neither had his father, and they'd been hunting in that region all their lives. The guide was dumbfounded at the wolf's presence at camp. So was Reggie, and he made it quite clear that this was a most happy event. He said wolves were out of control in the area, and were impacting many big game herds, especially caribou.

We skinned the wolf quickly and hung the hide up in a tree, and then continued on our journey toward caribou country. We had to hurry because we'd lost some valuable daylight dealing with the wolf.

For some reason, this wolf decided to approach camp. Jim Zumbo was extremely lucky -- few hunters ever see a wolf.

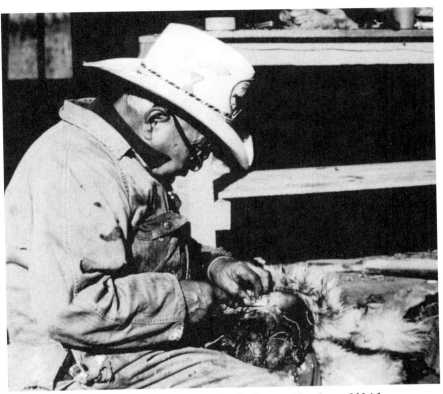

Legendary native, Alex Jack, fleshes author's wolf hide.

Several hours later, after a long horseback ride through rugged drainages, we made it to the top. It was time to break up into two parties. We were just about to decide who was going where, when Reggie spotted a bunch of caribou. When he pointed them out, I looked but initially couldn't see them. Finally, after closer observation, I made them out. I had never seen caribou in that country before and didn't know exactly what to look for, but the animals were out in the huge icefields and looked like vegetation.

Presently Reggie spotted another herd off in a different direction. Mike and I flipped a coin, deciding which way we were going. Reggie and I headed off in one direction, while Mike, Susan and their guide headed off in the other. We planned to rendezvous several hours later at the same spot where we had split up.

After riding for about an hour and a half, Reggie and I got up on the herd of caribou he'd initially spotted. The animals were fairly close, about 300 yards away, when we rode into view. They didn't seem to be terribly concerned with our presence. As Reggie explained, they didn't have any natural enemies that walked upright. Wolves and grizzlies were the big predators on caribou.

In order to get closer, we dismounted and walked alongside our horses and used them as shields. The ruse worked. The caribou didn't seem to mind the presence of the horses, so we were able to close the gap to within about 150 yards. One of the caribou in the bunch was a very good bull, and it didn't take a second look to know he was a dandy. Reggie and I quickly discussed the eligibility of the animal, and I told him it was perfectly fine for me.

I laid down in the snow using a rock for a rest, and put the caribou down. It was a beautiful animal, not big enough to make the record book, but nonetheless it was a handsome trophy.

With the animal caped, horns removed, and meat boned, we loaded the pack horses and headed back to meet up with Mike and Susan.

They were all smiles when we got back together, and the reason was immediately obvious. Mike had killed an absolutely fantastic caribou, one that would place high in the record book. Congratulations were in order and Reggie mentioned the fact that Mike won the bull because of a flip of a coin. This was not the first time I'd lost a chance at a great animal because of a coin flip. Since then I've said to heck with flipping coins.

We got back into camp just before dark and prepared to leave the next morning. My hunt was over. A moose and caribou were plenty of reasons to be delighted, but the wolf added an incredible bonus. I couldn't have been happier.

Heading out the next day was not without incident. Would you believe my horse and I did a repeat performance at the swamp? Once again, my horse was the only one that went through the muck, and this time I almost didn't get away without serious injury. As I had done before, I jumped out of the stirrups, but when the horse tried to get up it rolled across my legs.

Luckily, there was not a solid bottom underneath my legs, and the weight of the horse simply pushed me further down into the muck rather than breaking or tearing me apart. I was most happy about that.

Author is all smiles as he poses with a fine caribou -- but he lost out on the bigger bull because of a coin flip.

When we got to main camp, one of the Indians who was working for the Collingwoods offered to flesh out my wolf hide. Being a former trapper myself, and always having a fascination for working with hides, I was eager to watch.

I was most interested in this particular Indian. His name was Alex Jack and as I understand it, he was chief of his tribe. He had a beautifully weather-beaten face, a ruddy complexion, and you knew just by looking that he was a person who had survived many ordeals in the north country. I watched with rapt attention as Alex fleshed the wolf expertly. When he was done there was not a trace of fat, flesh, or muscle on the hide.

I flew out the next day, loaded with my trophies and a good share of the meat. The rest of the meat, which I couldn't fly out, was donated to the natives.

It had been a most memorable hunt. Some day I'd like to go back, this time hunting for a stone sheep, a mountain goat, and a grizzly. And I guarantee I'll have a black bear tag in my pocket when I return.

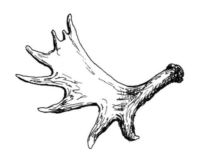

FORGET THE TEA
AND FOLLOW THE BOATS

Picture yourself somewhere in the Arctic Ocean, aboard a canoe. It's practically pitch black out, and you're floating along an uncharted shoreline.

"Where the hell are we?" one of my companions asked as our Inuit guide eased the freighter canoe slowly amidst the jagged rocks. As you might expect, there was some reason to be concerned.

At least Vin and I were. Salamonie Jaw, our Inuit guide, told us in broken English that there was nothing to fear. He'd find camp in short order.

A few moments later, the canoe slammed into a rock. It wasn't a wrenching blow that knocked us out of our seats, but more of an abrupt thud that put us at instant alert. A quick check with a flashlight revealed no damage to the canoe, but the incident didn't exactly add to our confidence level in terms of locating camp.

Salamonie continued piloting the canoe, guided by an intuitive Eskimo instinct that allowed him to navigate through the rocks. He was doing almost a perfect job. Almost.

A tense hour passed when Salamonie pointed off in the distance.

25

"Camp," he said.

The word came out as though he was asking someone to pass the ketchup.

Vin and I were not in such a tranquil mood. The discovery of our camp area was a whole lot more exciting to us.

"Where!" we both asked in unison.

Salamonie calmly pointed; we saw his arm extended in the faint starlight and looked. Sure enough, something was indeed out there in the dark. A couple small yellow dots suggested lantern lights, but it was so far away, and there were so many rocks in the underwater reefs around us, that we were still in for a mini-adventure before we climbed out of the canoe.

"Camp not far," Salamonie said, as if he'd read my mind. "Dark make things look far."

Good news. Salamonie was right, of course. I'd appreciated that phenomenon most of my adult life, but you need to constantly remind yourself that things really aren't as distant as they look at night.

Our canoe nudged against a few more rocks, and finally we were in open water, headed for camp. I was amazed, because Salamonie had never been to that area in his life. Yet, he unerringly charted a course through the reefs and found camp. It was a superb demonstration of the Inuit's sense of direction.

This trip so far had all the makings of a major nightmare, and Vin and I wondered aloud many times if we'd ever get out of there in one piece. More than once we were ready to say to heck with this caribou hunt.

We were on Baffin Island, hunting the Central Barren Ground caribou. According to Jerome Knap, our outfitter, our party was the first group of American hunters to ever hunt on Baffin Island; a fact that explained some of the problems we encountered.

Our group sat in on an orientation meeting in Montreal prior to the trip. During that meeting, Vin Sparano, OUTDOOR LIFE's editor, and I met Madleine Kay, a California jeweler who specializes in creating wildlife pieces.

Since Madleine didn't know anyone in the party, but she and I knew some mutual friends, she asked if she could share a tent with Vin and I. These were fairly large tents of the type used in the Arctic, and Madleine wasn't terribly interested in living in one solo.

At this point I must add that Madleine's pulchritudinous assets are downright phenomenal; the lady could easily be a centerfold in Playboy. Of course, Vin and I were pleased to accommodate her request, and so it was that we became an inseparable trio for the rest of the journey.

Freighter canoes like this one transported hunters 80 miles across Arctic ocean.

The hunt began at Cape Dorset, a small Inuit community on Baffin Island. As soon as we flew in, we immediately went to the shore where we'd be assigned an Inuit guide. Jerome chose Salamonie as our guide because he was the only one who spoke some English. Being writers, Vin and I hoped to be teamed up with an Inuit with whom we could communicate.

Our canoe was powered by a 35 hp outboard. Its generous 24-foot length and six-foot beam comfortably held the four of us, including our gear. Salamonie seemed to be an affable young man with an easy smile and a fair hand at speaking English. Most importantly, he seemed competent enough to get us to our destination, which was 80 miles away; all of it across the Arctic Ocean.

An elderly Inuit who was designated as chief took the lead. His canoe was trailed by six others, each carrying hunters and gear. We totaled seven Inuits and 18 hunters in all.

As we left the rocky coast, I assumed we'd all be traveling in a party so each canoe was visible. After all, that only made good sense, because several of the Inuit guides had never been to the area where we were going, including Salamonie. Good sense, however, isn't exactly a quality that's seen much in the far North. This isn't a negative critique of the Eskimo people, but a look at reality. As we soon learned, they are so incredibly rugged and self-reliant that they don't use logic in the manner we do.

This native appears to be quite happy with his mode of transportation. He was one of the few inhabitants of Cape Dorset on Baffin Island.

We'd gone about 10 miles, each canoe a small spot on the ocean; some in front of us and some behind. As we traveled, the canoes became farther and farther apart. Salamonie made no attempt to close the gap; he was perfectly content to do his own thing. The journey itself seemed to be questionable as far as the time factor was concerned. When we asked how long it would take at the outset of the trip, the Inuits threw their hands in the air. It appeared that the weather would dictate our travel time, which, of course, is always a factor on any hunting trip requiring a lengthy journey.

At some point that afternoon, Salamonie decided it was time to take a tea break. In the north, tea replaces coffee, and is the traditional drink.

When the guide pointed the canoe toward a rocky bay and left the parade of other canoes, I thought perhaps he wanted to gas up or take a nature break. But when Salamonie beached the canoe and calmly set up a pot on a small propane burner on the canoe floor, I was a mite concerned.

"What are we doing, Salamonie?" I asked pleasantly.

"We drink tea," he responded. "Time for tea."

Noting that all the canoes were now well ahead of us, I asked the obvious question. "Do you know where we're going?" I queried.

"No," he responded simply, and that was that.

Now I was carefully weighing my words, because it was necessary that the Inuit comprehend the next point.

"If you don't know where we're going," I said, "shouldn't we be following the other canoes?"

Salamonie digested that bit of information, and then it appeared that a light went on in his head.

"You right," he said. "No time for tea."

At that our guide put away the tea makings, fired up the outboard, and we were once again cruising along the ocean, but this time the other canoes were barely visible. They were just tiny dots in the huge expanse of sea that was now beginning to come alive. A stiff breeze came up, creating whitecaps and significant rollers. Suddenly the big 24-foot craft didn't seem so big anymore as we pitched and lurched in the growing waves.

Shortly afterward, we passed an island that was nothing but a pile of rocks. Surprisingly, a bunch of dogs appeared and ran along the waterline, barking incessantly. This was a sight worth pondering: what were a dozen dogs doing on a small, barren island.

Vin touched Salamonie on the shoulder and pointed to the dogs. The guide seemed to know what the question was going to be.

"Dogs free on island," he said. "Not free in town. Always tied up."

"What do they eat?" Madleine asked.

Salamonie shrugged. "Anything," he said. "Every few days somebody brings fish or bones or garbage. Dogs eat good."

Now the rollers grew stronger. The wind picked up considerably, and I began to wonder how much punishment the canoe would take as it rose and fell with the demands of the sea.

Soon Salamonie turned the craft away from the open ocean and headed toward a rocky island. The rest of our party had already pulled up to shore and were breaking out gear as we arrived.

"Sea too strong," Salamonie said. "We stay here until it get quiet."

That was perfectly fine with us.

It didn't take long to set up the tent. As added insurance, we tied large rocks all the way around in preparation for the storm that we were expecting. The Inuits are big on radio communications; there was a constant chatter between our camp and other groups scattered in the northland. A serious blow was in the forecast.

The wind increased during the night to the point where I wondered if our tent would stay erect. Vin, Madleine and I were quite comfortable, tucked in warm sleeping bags with a kerosene heater to warm the shelter.

Sometime during the night I felt a serious breeze on my face. A gap in the tent wall had opened, allowing the cold air in. The wind was now almost gale force, tearing at the ropes and fabric with mighty gusts. Vin and I worked to repair the tent wall, and I can recall the eerie feeling as I toiled outside. Illuminated in the starlight were the rest of the tents, each of them protecting humans inside. The ocean raged a few yards away, and the wind seethed through our remote outpost. It amazed me that we were where we were, toughing out a storm that would have killed us if we didn't have proper shelters. Indeed, the Inuits were survivors.

That point was driven home even more clearly the next day when our entire group of guides left camp in two boats, leaving the rest of us to wonder what in hell was going on. The wind had subsided some, but not enough to risk taking on the rest of the journey, especially a 25 mile crossing that would move us through an enormous open-water area with no islands to run to in case of danger. The crossing would have to be made in reasonably calm water.

Native mothers carry their infants on their backs in traditional style.

We heard distant shots a couple hours after the guides had left, but we had no clue what they were up to. They finally showed up several hours later, the bows of their canoes splatting the heaving ocean swells as they made their way back to our island.

Salamonie nonchalantly told us what they'd done.

"We shoot geese and ducks," he said, "and cook them in pot. Good stuff."

After further inquiry, the Inuit told us that he and his pals had killed some waterfowl, tossed them in a pot of boiling water, feathers and innards and all, and ate them after they had cooked a bit.

The fact that the Inuits left all their puzzled hunters in camp without any explanation of their plans made no difference. For all we knew, we were abandoned forever on the island. Interesting people, these Inuits. I was liking them more and more as time passed.

Salamonie pulled a stunt the next day that I still rave about to friends. Underway to our hunting camp once again, he'd spotted some ducks crossing in front of the canoe. He grabbed a very rusted .22 that leaned against the gunwale, and drew a bead on one of the ducks.

Mind you, we are in a craft that's crashing down from one wave to the other. The Inuit is using a rifle that looks like it sunk with the Titanic. You can imagine our astonishment when the little .22 bullet hit the duck smartly and sent it plummeting into the ocean.

Vin Sparano with his caribou. Vin was first in author's party to score.

Vin, Madleine, and I looked at each other in amazement. Never in my life had I seen such an incredible shot. We retrieved the duck and continued on our way.

Soon it was time to cross the big bay. Luck was on our side, since the ocean had calmed somewhat and the crossing was easily accomplished. Icebergs drifted about, and seals romped around our boat. A couple hunters had seal tags, but none were able to connect. I was disappointed, because I wanted to see how the seals were processed by the Inuits.

Finally we neared camp. As we pulled up to the shore, a small bunch of bull caribou ran off over a little rise. Some of the hunters could stand it no longer, and despite a bit of advice to hold off until bigger bulls were spotted, they had none of it. Fifteen minutes later several shots rang out; the hunt was over for a half dozen hunters who'd scored on mediocre bulls.

Since it was late in the day when we arrived, we set up camp and were in no hurry to hunt. The next morning would come soon enough.

As we cruised away from camp just after sunup, a lone bull appeared in the tundra close to shore. Salamonie gave the thumbs-up sign, but we weren't too sure. We'd been told that the Inuits had no experience in trophy hunting -- to them a small bull or cow or calf was prime meat. They seldom killed older bulls, and since we were the first hunters they'd ever guided, they weren't into evaluating antlers.

Nonetheless, the bull looked fine to us, and Vin made a stalk. His bull was down soon afterward, and we loaded it into the canoe after dressing it.

Salamonie, Madleine and I made a trek overland, and Vin tagged along as an observer. Suddenly I saw a tree branch in the bottom of a steep slope, but the thought occurred to me that there were no trees in the tundra. A bull caribou emerged; the branch was an antler. Another bull appeared, and both looked very good.

Figuring our hunt was over, Madleine and I stalked close. I suggested she shoot first and take the bull of her choice, but she declined.

"Not good enough," she said. "I'll bet we can do better."

I was amazed, but I trusted her judgment. As an artist who

created caribou images as well as other big game, she was schooled in antler configuration. I wasn't about to challenge her opinion.

We took off in the canoe to try another area, this time splitting up. I went off alone, while Vin accompanied Madleine and Salamonie.

Vin, Madleine, and I pose with our bulls.

I'd just reached the top of a ridge when a caribou jumped up and took off. My instinct was to shoot, simply because a running animal often clouds one's judgment and stimulates the adrenaline. I couldn't resist, and put the animal down.

Fifteen minutes later I heard a shot from Madleine's direction. She'd scored too, but her bull was fantastic. As we learned later, it was the best among our party, which was an outstanding accomplishment.

With the caribou loaded in the canoe, we were beset with another dilemma. The tide was out, and there was no way to move the canoe to the waterline, even if we emptied it. Without a load it still weighed close to a half ton.

When the tide finally rose to meet the canoe several hours later, we were on our way, but our journey to camp would be in the dark. As I described at the beginning of the chapter, Salamonie expertly piloted the canoe through the rocks and we safely reached camp that night.

Later that evening, as was the case every evening, a couple Inuit guides came into our tent. No knocking, no greetings – nothing – they just came in. Then they'd sit for a while and stare at the three of us as we either played cards, cleaned rifles, or made small talk. To this day I have no idea what prompted this surveillance; perhaps they'd never seen such a beautiful woman before, or perhaps they couldn't figure why she was sharing a tent with two men. Or maybe they believed we'd offer her to them. Whatever the case, it was most amusing. I regret I didn't have a translator around to interpret what they were saying when they came over for their nightly visits.

When it was time to pack up and leave, we made another interesting discovery. Behind the tent the Inuits lived in was a large pile of raw, meatless caribou ribs. Evidently they'd eaten the rib meat as a delicacy. This was further proof of the survival skills of the Inuits.

Salamonie made a most distressing announcement as we loaded the canoe.

"Maybe not have enough gas to get home," he said with amazing calmness.

"What should we do?" I said, noting that several other canoes, some of which held extra gas, were taking off for the 80 mile journey.

"My brother maybe have more gas," Salamonie said.

I had no idea Salamonie's brother was among our party.

"Where's your brother?" I asked.

Salamonie looked at the remaining Inuits who hadn't left yet, and then gazed out into the ocean.

"Out there," Salamonie responded, pointing to a boat half a mile distant racing away. We'd never catch up, since we had another half hour's work to do before we could leave.

It occurred to me that Salamonie hadn't done any advance thinking about the issue of inadequate gas, but he had a solution that might work.

"If we make it through cut with tide high, we maybe get home," he said. "If tide low and we have to go around, we don't get home. Run out of gas."

"Then what?"

Salamonie had no answer. He simply shrugged.

The cut was actually a 15-yard gap in a 20 mile-long peninsula. Making it through the cut should have been a top priority, but Salamonie wasn't in much of a hurry as he readied the canoe and lashed down the gear.

Madleine with her fine bull. The best taken on the trip.

Rain pelted us hard as we finally got under way, and I kept looking at the high tide mark on the distant shoreline. This adventure was not quite over.

At last the cut appeared and Salamonie finally expressed some emotion.

"Aieeeee," he said. "Maybe not make it. Tide too low."

Vin and I and Madleine looked at each other. It was almost humorous, but we weren't laughing.

This youngster possibly never had a new knife
-- until I gave him mine.

"We try anyway," Salamonie said with a big grin. "Maybe get across."

We tried, and we made it, though the prop cleared the rocks by a mere inch or two. Five minutes later and we wouldn't have cleared the cut.

About 10 miles from camp, Salamonie pointed to a small rocky island that couldn't have been more than a quarter mile long. He smiled, with a sort of distant look that we didn't understand.

"I born there," he said with pride.

Shaking my head in awe, I couldn't help but be impressed with this rugged lifestyle. These people were survivors, living in some of the harshest environment our planet has to offer.

Closer to the village, Salamonie talked about the Inuckshooks that looked down from high ridges. These were rocks piled high, constructed by Eskimos many generations ago to guide travelers along the myriad of islands and reefs.

Perhaps the most indelible sight, one which I failed to record with my camera, was a family of Inuits returning from a seal hunt. As they slowly approached the shore with a dead seal draped over the bow, other villagers ran down amidst barking dogs and shouting youngsters. The look of pride on the faces of the victorious hunters was a beautiful sight, each of them beaming and gesturing toward the seal.

Later, when we were standing around in a small group, I noted a young boy looking at me as I whittled on a small caribou rib bone with my pocket knife. He seemed mesmerized by the knife and couldn't take his eyes off it.

Impulsively I closed the blade and offered the knife to the boy. He looked at the knife, then into my eyes, and seemed confused. I gestured with the knife, extending it toward him, but he still couldn't comprehend my intentions. An old man standing next to the boy who might have been his grandfather took the boy's hand and held it toward the knife. I placed it in the boy's hand and saw a look of total joy and happiness in his face. At that he took the knife, shot me a huge grin, and ran off as fast as he could to show it to his pals.

I, too, had a big smile on my face, and I'll never forget the total sense of satisfaction I had when the boy accepted the knife. It had been a fitting end to a memorable arctic adventure with an incredible race of human beings. I had a tough time getting on the plane. My visit in that wonderful land had been far too short.

THE HONEYMOON HUNT

I was a nervous wreck. The bull caribou was 200 yards away, moving slowly through heavy brush. My wife rested the .270 on a branch, drew a careful bead, and I finally kept quiet. Up to that point I'd been coaching her: "Get a steady hold, take a deep breath, squeeze the trigger," and so on. Now it was time for the conclusion of a long-anticipated hunt.

You might say I was profoundly astounded when Madonna agreed to spend our honeymoon in a hunting camp. During our courtship, I'd carefully avoided suggesting that she try hunting. If the whim ever struck her to do so, it would come from some influence other than mine. I didn't want her to feel obligated or pressured, though I secretly hoped that she'd some day become a hunter.

I suppose that Henri Poupart had something to do with her decision. A jolly French Canadian, Henri is the owner of Safari

Nordik, an outfitting firm that specializes in Quebec caribou hunts. We met Henri at the International Sportsmen's Expo in Sacramento, California, and it didn't take him long to convince Madonna and I that a far north adventure would offer a splendid honeymoon.

A herd of caribou swims across a bay close to camp.

Madonna wasn't certain that she wanted to hunt on the trip, but since most of the caribou camps were close to good fishing, she'd be able to fish to her heart's content if she opted not to hunt. She is crazy about fishing.

When we initially planned our honeymoon, I asked if she'd like to go on a Caribbean cruise or a trip to the tropics.

"No way," she responded, "and you know better than to ask."

Indeed I did, but I was just covering the bases. She had a special attraction for the far north, as I did. Palm trees were out; the tundra was in. Henri's offer was the perfect solution.

Madonna was born and raised in Denver. Neither her Dad nor two brothers hunted, and she never fired a gun until she met me. She enjoyed the sessions on the gun range, starting with a .22, working up to a .243, and then a .30/06.

She admitted that shooting was fun, but was initially hesitant to take the step into hunting. She enjoyed cooking and eating wild game as much as I did, and reasoned that I was perfectly capable of keeping the freezer stocked.

The summer prior to our Quebec adventure was a time of madness. Between building a log home in the Wyoming mountains and planning a wedding, we had no time to prepare for the trip. There wasn't even an hour to fish a trout stream near our home.

Despite the time crunch, we took some time off to hunt prairie dogs. Madonna had been leaning more and more toward hunting on our honeymoon, but she didn't want to try it until she actually participated on a hunt. I was in total agreement, since she needed to be initiated into the sport before the Canadian trip.

Madonna glasses for caribou. We used a boat to get from camp to the hunting areas.

Using the .270 Kimber she'd hunt caribou with, she nicely eliminated some pesky prairie dogs in an area where they were a nuisance. She had no reservations or misgivings before or after she squeezed the trigger. The pressure was off, and she was ready for the Canada trip.

These bulls allowed us to get fairly close. This is a great bowhunting area.

The flight from Montreal to Henri's jump-off point in Kuujuac was as I'd expected. As usual, I was immensely impressed with the barren look of the landscape that unfolded beneath the 737 jetliner. Literally thousands of lakes, ponds, and rivers, many of them unnamed, were splashed into tundra that was total wilderness. Much of that incredibly remote country had never been walked upon by a human being.

Madonna's impressions paralleled mine. She'd never been to Quebec before, but had fished extensively in Alaska, where the same type of seemingly barren tundra stretched away into what appeared to be infinity.

From Kuujuac (formerly called Fort Chimo), which is an isolated Inuit village, Madonna and I flew to our hunting camp with Henri and his partner Johnny May, a legendary bush pilot in Quebec. Johnny pointed out various features as we flew, including a number of caribou that dotted the tundra below.

Henri made a friendly wager that we'd handily collect our two bulls each in rapid order, and I hoped he was right. Moreover, I was hoping for a flawless trip, one that would encourage Madonna to want to continue hunting.

We were just one day into the caribou hunt when we spotted several bulls from our boat as we headed down the lake away from camp. After carefully beaching the boat, Madonna, our guide, and I made a stalk on four bulls that worked their way through thick brush.

I'd thought about Madonna's first-ever shot dozens of times before the hunt, rolling it over and over in my mind. It had to be perfect.

Because we'd climbed a steep hill to where the caribou were, we were out of breath when she had an opportunity to shoot. The rest wasn't solid, her stance wasn't ideal, and she missed.

It was like a bad dream, but the bullet that flew over the caribou's back was real. Madonna wasn't sure what to do next, but the caribou offered no second shot, disappearing rapidly into the vegetation with the other three bulls in the herd.

We hiked on. A few minutes later I spotted a lone bull feeding in a small basin about 150 yards away. This was a very good bull; much better than the one she'd missed.

Madonna centered the crosshairs of her rifle on the bull and fired, this time with a comfortable rest. I was instantly relieved. It was a perfect hit; the animal went down immediately at the shot.

My worst fears never materialized. A miss was acceptable, but a crippling shot might have turned her away from hunting for good.

Madonna's reaction to the dead animal was one of curiosity and satisfaction. She accepted her responsibility as a hunter, helping us dress and quarter the carcass.

I took a bull soon afterward, and by midday we had all eight quarters hanging in the meat shed at camp. It had been a fine day.

The next day, Madonna was presented with another dilemma. She put her second bull down with a well-placed round, but the animal required a finishing shot. I offered to do it for her, but Madonna shook her head and approached the fallen bull with resolve and determination. It was an unpleasant chore, but one which she accepted in her role as a hunter. After her bull was dressed, I also shot my second caribou.

With four caribou quartered and hung in the meat shed, Henri and Johnny offered to take us fishing. We didn't hesitate to go. Johnny, who is part Inuit and one of the top bush pilots in Quebec, knew where all the good spots were.

Madonna shows off one of her two big bulls. Not bad for her first hunt.

We soon taxied off the lake, headed for one of Johnny's fishing holes. Soon we landed along a large river – the same river where thousands of caribou had drowned when an upstream dam spilled too much water during the annual caribou migration. I'd read about the tragedy in the news, and had no idea where the river was located in Quebec. Now we were fishing it.

It didn't take long to catch a variety of trout, but Johnny was hankering to try another spot. We soon learned why.

After landing on a small lake, we hiked up a river toward another lake that flowed into the river. Johnny and Henri opted to fish the river, and suggested that Madonna and I try the upriver lake. They also warned us to take plenty of bug dope. I'm glad we paid attention and complied.

Madonna's first cast into the lake produced a jolting strike.

She fought a big fish, and I couldn't believe my eyes when I identified it as a huge brookie. Before releasing it, I estimated it to be at least six pounds. My next cast also resulted in a hard strike, and this time I landed another fine brook trout that was probably close to five pounds.

I must mention here that the biggest brook trout I'd seen in a lifetime of fishing was a four and a half pounder caught in Maine. My personal largest was three pounds.

The action continued, and Johnny showed up, grinning from ear to ear. He unhooked a few of our fish, tossed them up on the bank, and I assumed he was going to take them to his family. The Inuit people abide by different regulations and natural laws because their lifestyle requires them to hunt and fish for much of their food.

After we caught several more trout, Johnny gathered up the few he kept, strung them on an alder branch, and presented them to Madonna and I.

"Enjoy these with your caribou dinners," he said simply with a smile. "And don't be concerned about killing them. No one fishes this spot but me, and I fish it every 10 years or so. Besides,

Henri Poupart, Madonna, and Johnnie May are all smiles after we fished for big brookies.

there are hundreds of places just like it, unnamed places that have never been fished."

With the trip coming to a climax, we prepared our caribou meat and trout for the long journey back to Wyoming. Everything arrived home in excellent condition, and during the months that followed, we enjoyed the superb caribou venison and trout fillets, reminiscing frequently about the Quebec adventure.

To my relief, the hunt had gone off almost perfectly, and there was no doubt in my mind that Madonna would be a regular hunting companion. No longer would she say to heck with hunting.

She made that point perfectly clear as the caribou meat began slowly disappearing from the freezer, suggesting that perhaps an elk or mule deer hunt might be next on our outdoor calendar.

I, of course, quickly agreed, and hunting suddenly took on a new meaning. Elk season couldn't come quickly enough.

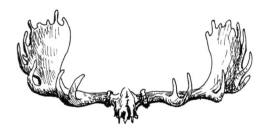

WHEN PAT McMANUS
DIDN'T TELL A FIB

I've always had a special fascination for antelope. They aren't the wariest of all our big game animals, and it's easy to see them, but they're so unique and so exclusively western that they have a distinctive appeal. That's not to say they're always easy to hunt. Several of my antelope hunts are chronicled in this book; many were no piece of cake.

Perhaps I hold antelope in high esteem because they were the first animals I'd seen on my first journey West. I was riding on a bus during the fall of 1960, headed to Utah where I'd study forestry at Utah State University. I had just left my home state of New York, and until that bus ride, had hardly been more than 200 miles from home. I was so excited about seeing the West I could hardly stand myself.

Imagine my unbridled joy when I looked out the window of the bus at sunup and saw a bunch of peculiar animals. Recognizing them instantly as antelope, I woke up the passenger who was dozing alongside me and told him the good news. He grunted and went back to snoring, no doubt figuring he was seated next to a wacky kid.

Merritt Benson, former staff editor with OUTDOOR LIFE, glasses for antelope from a high vantage point.

My first antelope hunt was in Utah and is recounted in another chapter, but the majority of my hunting for the prairie speedsters has been in Wyoming. I moved here in 1985, but have been hunting antelope as a nonresident for years prior to moving to the Cowboy State.

The area near Elk Mountain, which is southeast of Rawlins and just south of Interstate 80, is one of my favorite spots on the planet. A number of my deer and antelope hunts have taken place within sight of the mountain.

My first hunt in the area was on my own. My son Dan went along, and at 12 wasn't yet old enough to hunt big game. I'm not sure if Dan enjoyed our first trip because he wanted to observe the hunt, or because I let him drive our hunting rig on the expansive prairie. I suspect it was more of the latter. A 12-year old kid drives wherever and whenever he can.

Another hunt was with a trio from a southern state; I can't remember which. It was a fine hunt, with all of us coming up with 14-inch antelope. We hunted both private and public land, and I was amazed at the willingness of many of the ranchers to allow us free trespass. One rancher had a fresh pot of coffee on his porch, and we always felt at home.

The Virginian Hotel in nearby Medicine Bow is a prominent landmark in the area, and one which we frequented as much as possible. The hotel has a wonderful, authentic saloon, a decent restaurant, and the rooms are just the way they were back around the turn of the century. The old hotel and Medicine Bow were made famous by Owen Wister in his novel, THE VIRGIN-IAN. Legend has it that while playing poker the small town's deputy sheriff, James Davis, was called an insulting canine name by another player. Reportedly, Davis' response was, "When you call me that, smile." Those words, overheard by hotel guest, Owen Wister, were immortalized.

One particular hunt was most noteworthy, in that my buddies had involved me in a bit of a scam with some of the local ladies. It happened that the boys showed up a day before I did, and met some gals in the hotel restaurant. When my pals learned that Medicine Bow has an annual Can-Can festival and the gals were dancers, they decided to have a little fun – at my expense. The bums told the women that a hotshot reporter for a travelogue magazine was coming to town and suggested that the ladies dress in full costume so their pictures could be taken when the bigshot arrived. You guessed it – I was supposed to be that bigshot, but I had no idea of the ruse.

The ladies thought it was a great idea, and agreed to meet up at the hotel a couple hours after my arrival. I might add that the women were not the sleazy type, but wholesome gals who enjoyed participating in the festival for their little town.

I arrived close to schedule and was immediately approached by a hotel employee who asked my identity. When I introduced myself, I was whisked off to the pool room where the boys were having a big time playing eight-ball. They could hardly wait to tell me the great news, and at first I balked. No way was I going to be an impostor.

They worked on me for awhile until I softened. Though I'm an outdoor writer reporting on hunting and fishing, I had done some travel articles in the past. A story about a small festival in Wyoming might fly after all.

Bob Mosley, me and Parker Davies show off our antelope.

The girls showed up on time, dressed in their Can-Can costumes. I ripped off a half dozen rolls of film, but not until I told the gals the truth. They went along with it in good-natured fashion, and we took the bunch of them out to dinner at a great restaurant near Elk Mountain.

On another hunt, I was joined by Leon Parson and a pal, both from Idaho. Leon is a very well-known artist, having painted several dozen covers for OUTDOOR LIFE as well as numerous other beautiful works. He's one of my favorite artists, and I've enjoyed his company on hunting and fishing trips.

While we ate lunch at the Virginian restaurant one day, Leon was busy drawing on a napkin. When we were done eating, Leon handed me the napkin and told me to keep it. He'd drawn a beautiful pencil sketch of a mule deer.

Damn! I finally had a Parson original! I was mighty proud of it, and carefully placed it in the glove box of my truck. A couple weeks later, I needed a bit of cloth to wipe the oil from the dipstick. Yes, I did it -- having forgotten what was on the napkin stashed in my glove compartment. I ruined my original and still haven't forgiven myself to this day.

An unhappy hunt occurred one year when I hunted the Medicine Bow area with two doctor pals of mine from Utah, Parker Davies and Bob Mosley. We scouted extensively and had located several good bucks prior to the season, including a dandy animal that I was convinced would go 16 inches. I'd yet to get a 16-inch buck.

Bob had his heart set on a fine 15-inch buck he'd spotted that had wide prongs and massive bases. Parker and I would try for the big one, provided he was in the area where we'd seen him last.

We spotted the big buck at 8 a.m. Our plan was to move in on the antelope from opposite directions; hopefully one of us would get a shot. The buck was in the middle of a flat prairie with no opportunity to sneak close.

Two hours later, I was belly-crawling commando-style with my rifle cradled in my arms. I didn't know where Parker was, but I managed to get within 400 yards of the buck by staying in a shallow gully. Another 50 yards and I'd set up for a shot.

Suddenly, a jeep roared over a rise and the occupants gave chase to the antelope herd that included the big buck. A series of shots rang out and the buck fell. The driver stopped next to the dead antelope.

I was seething, not because I'd been gypped out of a great buck, but by the horrid display of bad ethics. I walked over to the vehicle, telling myself to bite my tongue, otherwise I'd have said a whole lot more than I intended. Parker was also walking over to the rig.

We got there just as a man finished measuring the horns.

"Sixteen plus on each side," he announced proudly, "and this is my boy's first buck. He's a happy kid."

The youngster was all smiles, and obviously had no idea that shooting an animal from a moving vehicle was wrong, violating a major principle of hunting ethics. I didn't have anything nice to say, and I knew if I offered my feelings, the boy's relationship with his Dad might be adversely affected, so I kept my mouth shut. Parker and I left, amazed at the father's values.

The hunt went well for us, however. Bob got his nice 15 incher, and Parker and I scored on big bucks, too, but I'll always

Taking an antelope with a handgun, as Jim Zumbo shows here, is often tough because of the difficulty in getting close.

remember that vehicle roaring after the antelope.

Without question the most memorable Wyoming antelope hunts for me were those held for handicapped hunters. Sometime in the early 80's, I was visiting with Bill Brown, who at the time worked for the Rocky Mountain Conservation Fund, an organization that raised money for various conservation and wildlife projects. I happened to mention to Bill that I'd received a letter from a reader who was permanently paralyzed, and he wondered why there were no stories written for handicapped hunters, nor were there any special hunts available. I suggested that we consider sponsoring an antelope hunt for handicapped hunters, and Bill jumped on the idea like a cat on a mouse. Enlisting the aid of a bunch of great people, most of them from Douglas, Wyoming, we launched our first hunt. Gary and Jane Stearnes of Douglas, and Margaret Salisbury of Casper, who was director of the Wyoming Chapter of Multiple Sclerosis, were all instrumental in helping us get the hunt off the ground.

We didn't know what to expect on the first hunt. A dozen hunters arrived, all of them confined to wheelchairs; and some of them with more paralysis than others. Some had nerve diseases, or had had strokes, and many were war veterans or victims of accidents. The hunt went well, with everyone scoring, but I can tell you that at the awards banquet when each hunter wheeled up to the stage to accept an award, there were no dry handkerchiefs in the audience. Named the Helluva Hunt, it is one of the most satisfying programs I'd ever participated in, in my life. The hunt has now seen its 10th anniversary and is stronger than ever. Other states have picked up on the idea, and a fair number of handicapped hunters can enjoy an incredible experience.

I'd like to share two incidents. On the first hunt we had an elderly gentleman with advanced MS. His lower body was literally in a bag where he was hooked up to various tubes. We carefully lifted him into Gary's suburban, where he sat next to the passenger window. Gary drove, while Jane and I sat in the back. As we bounced over bumps, I held his shoulders to ease the shock.

When we spotted an antelope, we rested the rifle on a cushion out the window, and Gary pointed the gun toward the animal, moving it slowly until the hunter could see it in the scope. I held both my hands between the butt stock and the man's shoulder to protect him from the recoil, and Jane put her finger on the trigger. The man was so weak he couldn't pull the trigger. The plan was for the man to gently place pressure on Jane's finger when the crosshairs were correctly positioned on the antelope. It took three antelope and most of a day to get it right, but our efforts were rewarded with a big doe. I can assure you that Gary, Jane, and I had teary eyes throughout the whole experience, and not from the Wyoming wind, either. The man died a year later.

A happy hunter with his antelope taken during the handicapped Helluva Hunt.

I should mention that the Wyoming Game and Fish Commission enacted a special law enabling handicapped hunters to shoot from vehicles. Also, some of the antelope weren't terribly wary and allowed a fairly close approach because we hunted on opening weekend and the private lands we hunted were temporarily reserved for the handicapped hunters.

Another time we were escorting a hunter who was permanently paralyzed from an injury suffered while he was riding a bull in a rodeo. We lifted him out to his wheelchair, and wheeled him to a point where he could shoot into a draw. Gary and I made a big circle afoot while Jane stayed with the hunter. The plan was to run some antelope past the hunter.

It didn't work, and we returned to the vehicle, with me complaining because I'd been wearing cowboy boots since I hadn't intended to do much walking. If you aren't familiar with cowboy boots, I can assure you that they're not intended for walking over rocks.

"My feet are killing me," I said when I got in the back seat next to the hunter.

Just then I saw him glance down, and then quickly look out the window. What a jerk I'd been. I was complaining about my feet when this unfortunate man had no feet.

Nothing needed to be said at that moment but I had to apologize.

"I'm sorry," I said. "I wasn't thinking."

"No problem," was the man's response. "I understand."

Since those hunts, I've never again complained because a parking spot was reserved for the handicapped. Sometimes we don't consider how lucky we are when we're healthy.

One year a group of writers got together for a hunt that I'd put together near Elk Mountain, with cooperation from my friend, Ed Beattie, a fellow alumni from the same forestry school. At the time, Ed headed up Elk Mountain Safaris, a hunting concession that was made up of several ranches. Ed got permission for us to hunt some of that land, and we also hunted public land as well.

Our bunch consisted of Pat McManus, humor writer and best-selling author who writes the last page in OUTDOOR LIFE, Vin Sparano, who then was Executive editor of OUTDOOR LIFE, Bill Rooney, editor of AMERICAN FORESTS magazine, William (Harold) Nesbitt, who was then Executive Director of the Boone and Crockett Club, outdoor writer Kathy Etling and her husband Bob.

We had a borrowed motorhome, my camp trailer, and several vehicles, including one that Pat rented.

Upon their arrival at the campsite, there was a bit of grumbling about the spot I'd chosen. Pat spoke up and claimed that the area was so flat that one would have to walk over the horizon to make a call of nature. (The RV's had no water or bathroom facilities because they'd been winterized).

It went downhill from there, but we had many laughs, and some superb conversations around the campfire. We all got antelope, with Bill Rooney taking the biggest with 15-plus inch horns, and Vin making the longest shot. The animal was so far away I won't tell you the distance because you wouldn't believe it.

But it was Pat's antelope that was the most memorable. Pat was driving his rental vehicle, with Bill, Vin, and I along as observers. When we came to a very deep gully, Pat stopped and wondered out loud if his rig would make it, allowing as to how he'd only driven it a couple hundred miles. He suggested that maybe one of us would like to drive across the gully while he guided us through, but we politely reminded him that he was the only one insured for that rental. Realizing that he was about to lose face, Pat jumped behind the wheel, while the rest of us jumped out, explaining that it would take all of us to guide him.

Somehow Pat managed to negotiate the chasm, though we all were somewhat concerned with the status of the vehicle's undercarriage, since it carved a gouge in the earth where it plowed across. The vehicle seemed to be okay, however, and we were off to find Pat a big antelope.

Presently we spotted a buck in the distance. After hiding the vehicle in a depression, we watched as Pat took careful aim and fired. The bullet hit somewhere within five yards of the antelope (we think), and the darndest thing happened. The buck couldn't tell where the shot came from and ran closer to Pat. Again Pat fired, and again the bullet hit somewhere close to the animal, and once more the antelope ran toward Pat. As the buck continued on what appeared to be a suicide march, Pat kept on shooting, until he finally ended the antelope's charge and dropped it handily.

Pat claimed, of course, that he didn't want to hit the animal so far away because it would be unsporting, and he also might have picked up cactus needles in his vehicle's tires if he had to drive very far to load the animal. When we questioned the credibility of that statement, he fessed up and told us that there was a slight earth tremor every time he squeezed the trigger -- so imperceptible that the rest of us didn't feel it. Of course, we believed him.

Bill Rooney with the best antelope of our trip.

We could not, however, dispute the fact that Pat was indeed charged by an antelope, though the word "charged" might be stretching it a bit. Pat wrote a column about the hunt for OUT-DOOR LIFE, calling it, The Dumbest Antelope. I was glad to see that he incorporates a bit of truth in his column from time to time.

On the way home from that hunt, my pickup started spewing oil from somewhere around the oil tank. I was in the middle of nowhere when I discovered the problem, but was able to get to

Pat McManus, obviously uninjured, poses with the antelope that charged him.

a gas station. However, there was no mechanic around, so I bought four quarts of oil. Those quarts lasted for 30 miles, and I bought another four quarts. When the same thing happened again, I bought a whole case and managed to get home. Problems like that started happening regularly to that vehicle, so I said to heck with that pickup truck and traded it in for another one.

Living in Wyoming places a unique perspective on antelope hunting. You don't seem to get so excited and worked up as with other animals because when you leave the house in the morning, you know you're going to see animals; it's a matter of how big the buck will be and how close you can drive to it. I've taken two bucks on the way to the dump, which is not exactly much of a hunt.

When some out-of-state pals inquired about antelope hunting and seemed to be all concerned about finding animals I told them it was pretty easy, and allowed as to how I'd gotten a couple while headed to the dump.

So, my pal asked the obvious question: "Say, Jim, do you suppose you could give us directions to the dump?"

POWDER YOUR NOSE
BEFORE YOU SHOOT

Maaa--ke Up!

When my wife drew a Utah moose permit, I was enormously tickled. Having lived in Utah for about 15 years, I'd tried unsuccessfully to draw a tag. All that bad luck changed in 1994 when Madonna hit the lottery for the nonresident permit. The unit she drew was the north slope of the Uinta Mountains on the southern Wyoming border.

I'd done quite a bit of wandering about in that general area for years, and in fact had drawn a Wyoming moose tag just across the border from Madonna's unit about 10 years before. (It was a pretty sorry moose hunt; read about it elsewhere in this book). I knew a bit about her unit in Utah, having done some fishing and elk hunting there, but not enough to be comfortable about hunting it without some extensive scouting.

The first thing I did was to call a couple game warden buddies of mine in Utah who I'd known for years. They suggested a number of drainages, but all were fairly popular, and I figured we'd have plenty of company from other hunters. I believe about 20 tags were issued for the unit.

One particular spot seemed to hold some promise, a public piece of land that was accessible via private land. The trick was to get permission to trespass. I wasn't all that excited to do so, and Madonna agreed that she'd prefer shooting a moose on public land. If it turned out that hunting was poor, we might try the private piece if we could locate the landowners.

The area she drew has always been Utah's top moose producing area. Numbers are so high that many animals have been trapped over the years and restocked elsewhere to form brand-new moose populations.

We bought some Forest Service maps of the area and towed our camp trailer up into the mountains. It should have been a routine drive, but we experienced a frightening incident in the lowlands before we started to climb into the higher elevations. It was about 8 a.m. when I saw a car traveling at a high rate of speed toward us. The vehicle made it around a bad curve, but went off the road and the driver overcorrected. Fortunately, he maintained control and got the car back into his lane, but then he headed directly for us in our lane. A head-on seemed obvious, because there was no place for me to go, except down a steep embankment to the right. I was just about to ditch into the embankment, but the car suddenly swerved and narrowly missed us by inches. I'll never forget the look on the driver's face. Though I had only a split-second glance, he was grinning wildly and his eyes were glassy. No question that the fool was roaring drunk. Madonna and I took a while to compose ourselves. It had been a close call, and if I hadn't been towing the camper I'd have turned around and gotten their license plate number, or done something worse. I believe the local police would have been interested in talking to them.

We parked the Jayco camp trailer in a beautiful spot along a mountain lake, and headed out to scout the area. Around noon we drove into another campground and met two deputy sheriffs who were checking out a stolen canoe. We made some small talk, and I told them I wished I'd seen them sooner because I believed a couple drunks were on the loose.

"Not any more," said one of the deputies. "One of our officers spotted them weaving through town. They're now sleeping it off in the slammer. Evidently they'd been drinking all night at a party."

That was the best news I'd heard in a long time. I hoped the idiots would serve plenty of time, long enough to wipe off the ugly smile I'd seen on the driver.

With a good look at the road system and the willow bottoms, we left the camper behind for a few days. I had an elk hunt in Utah coming up, and Madonna would spend a few days with the kids in Salt Lake City. Then we'd return and begin the moose hunt on the opener.

The elk hunt was great; resulting in a dandy six-point bull, one of my best ever. I stored the meat in a locker, intending to return after Madonna's moose hunt. With luck, we'd have plenty of moose meat to add to the elk.

My son, Dan, and daughter, Angie, came up for opening weekend. If Madonna got her bull early, we'd have plenty of help getting it out. Also on the hunt was Debbie Williams who worked for George Taulman of United States Outfitters. George was instrumental in Madonna drawing a tag, since he's a licensing agent and applies us for many of our big game hunts. Debbie was going along as a photographer, hoping to chronicle the hunt for a new promotional video that George was producing. Debbie is from Maine, and in fact had done a great deal of moose hunting there. This was good, since she was no stranger to moose hunting and would know what to expect.

The first morning our gang headed to a prime spot that always held moose, according to my game warden sources. We eased along a willow-lined creek, but never saw a moose. At noon we tried another drainage; still no moose. Late in the afternoon we spotted three cows and one small bull. As a nonresident, Madonna could take only a bull, and this little guy wasn't at all tempting.

The next day was a repeat of the first. A number of cow moose were around, but still no bulls. A hunter on horseback was just descending from the high country, and he told us he'd seen three big bulls. Unfortunately, the moose were six miles or so up, and we had no horses. I was intending on using our one-wheeled carrier, and my most fervent hopes were that Madonna would take her moose fairly close to the truck. I knew from talking to sources that the biggest bulls were up high. The best we could expect in the lower elevations was a bull with a 30-inch spread. Madonna claimed that was perfectly fine for her, and I liked her attitude a whole lot.

Madonna with her moose. Happily, it fell close to the road.

Afterward we ran into an elk bowhunter who proved to be a friendly chap. As good luck would have it, he was related to the people who owned the piece of private land that we'd been told about. Indicating that the landowners often granted permission, he agreed to follow us into town and call them. He had to go into town for supplies anyway.

He obtained permission for us to hunt with no problem, and we planned to hunt the next day. Dan and Angie had to return to Salt Lake that evening.

Our trip to the private parcel was unrewarding though I saw a ton of moose droppings (well, almost), and there was no question that moose had been around. It was a most unique spot, since there wasn't a willow swamp for miles. Lodgepole pine and Douglas fir grew in the area, and for some reason the moose concentrated there. No big surprise, because the Shiras moose subspecies we hunted are fond of the forest, but I was at a loss to explain the heavy concentration of droppings. None seemed to be fresh, though we looked hard for several hours. I thought it wiser to return down to the willow bottoms, having a hunch that the moose used the forest area next to the private land later in the fall. The bowhunter told us he'd usually seen moose there during deer season which was mid-to late October, several weeks later.

More hiking through the willows was uneventful, though we continued to see cows here and there. Moose meat wasn't yet a reality, but we were nonetheless enjoying the hunt. This was beautiful country; Madonna thought it was among the nicest she'd hunted. That's saying something, because she was born in Colorado and we live in a gorgeous part of Wyoming.

Madonna trims away some of the fat from the moose carcass before we load it up.

Late one afternoon I spotted a cow moose in a willow swamp. I got out of the truck, as always when I saw a moose, and looked further.

There he was -- a bull moose with at least a 30-inch spread. Quickly we got out of the truck and made a sneak toward the bull. Debbie followed with the big movie camera.

The cow had us pegged. She stared intently, but the bull was behind some brush and wasn't yet aware of our presence. Madonna eased up to a tree, found a solid rest, and waited for the bull to move into the open. Debbie set the camera on a tripod, and we waited. It was the moose's move.

Presently the bull took three steps and he was in the clear. When Madonna fired, the bull ran forward 10 yards and collapsed.

It was a perfect shot. The 7mm Rem Mag bullet took the bull behind the shoulder, penetrating the rib cage and taking out the lungs. There was hardly a pound of meat wasted, since the bullet hit no big bones, but went in and out of the ribs. Furthermore, the bull dropped about three feet from a little creek, handy to water that would make the field-dressing easier.

With just a couple hours of daylight left, we set to work and dressed the bull. I skinned his neck to be sure to get the heat out where the hide was thickest. The nights were cool, getting down to 35 or 40.

The next morning I was happy to see frost in the little willow swamp. It was a few degrees cooler there than elsewhere, which is typical of bottoms. There was no frost anywhere else, at least between camp and the moose.

By noon the moose was history, completely skinned, quartered, and placed in heavy-duty meat sacks. With the one-wheeled carrier, Madonna and I got the moose to the truck, while Debbie photographed and pitched in to help at a steep incline.

As we prepared the camper to leave, we heard a ruckus in the lake behind us and saw a bull moose cavorting about. He was just a bit smaller than Madonna's, and I was glad she had her bull. Had she not, she might have been tempted to take this one, and if it had fallen in the lake we'd have had a monumental job of dressing and moving it. I haven't yet shot a moose in the water, but I've been around when it happened. I can tell you it's no fun; and I've made it perfectly clear to anyone in earshot that I'll never shoot a moose in the water. To heck with that kind of wet work!

THIS AIN'T YOUR ANTELOPE, MAX

But one of us ou'ta shoot 'em.

This is one for the "Stories Worth Retelling" Department. It's absolutely true (honest), as are all the stories in this book. It involves an antelope hunt I took several years ago with two friends, one experienced in antelope hunting, and the other inexperienced. In fact, it was the first big game hunt of his life for the latter. I'll change the names to spare embarrassment to the individuals involved. We'll call the experienced hunter Jake and the first-timer, Max.

Jake and I took Max to a good antelope spot in central Wyoming, and had high hopes because there were lots of antelope around. We were excited for Max, though a mite concerned because he hadn't had much time to shoot his brand new rifle. Jake and I also had antelope tags but we didn't intend to use them until Max scored first.

The opening day of the hunt was a typically beautiful September morning.

Right off the bat we spotted a nice buck antelope with 14 inch horns standing in a little depression. It was a perfect setup for Max, and the buck seemed unconcerned about our presence. How nice. We expected Max's hunt would be over in a few seconds.

Easing out of the pickup and sneaking a hundred yards to the top of the rise, Max used a fence post as a rest and took careful aim. We were right! The hunt was over in seconds as the antelope fell hard to the ground.

With my cameras in hand, I headed for the buck with Max while Jake walked over to the truck whereupon he'd drive to the antelope. I congratulated Max and allowed as to how he was a lucky hunter to have gotten such a fine antelope so quickly. He had made a good neck shot.

I asked Max to pose, and he bent down to hold up the buck's head while I focused my camera. Max was just about to grab a horn when the antelope wiggled. Max pulled back and the antelope started thrashing a bit. I assumed these were the death throes, but the animal kept moving about. Suddenly it got up on all fours with legs spread far apart and wobbled from side to side.

This was not like any death throe I'd ever seen, and I was at a loss for words when Max asked me what was going on. He'd never been around an animal that was either dead or supposed to be dead, as this one was. Frankly, I'd never seen one behave quite this way, either. I was as stupefied as Max.

Now the antelope managed to take a step, then another. Surely he would keel over any minute and that would be that. But the buck had other ideas. The animal appeared to be gaining strength, and worked toward the top of the rise. I stared in disbelief, still expecting it to go down.

All the while Max had his rifle ready, waiting for me to tell him to shoot. Since the antelope was just 10 yards away and I wasn't sure that Max could hit it again (Max was badly shaken, and shaking badly), I opted to wait a couple more moments. I just knew the buck would go down any second.

Dumb me.

A very nice pronghorn antelope. Note the heavy bases, prongs, and length of his horns.

Suddenly the buck seemed to regain all its senses and started to trot away.

"Shoot!" I said to Max.

Max chambered a round, or tried to do so, but in his nervous state he managed to jam the rifle. I grabbed it, but it was jammed pretty good. It would take some time to fix it.

So there we were, with a useless rifle, and a wounded antelope quickly putting distance between us. We watched, totally helpless and frustrated. I was simply amazed -- and feeling real stupid.

The buck had just disappeared over the rise when Jake drove up.

Antelope are said to run 55 mph. When chasing a doe, maybe he can do 60.

"Where's the buck?" he asked.

"It's gone," I stammered. "Just got up and took off!"

"Be serious," Jake said.

"I'm as serious as a heart attack," I answered. "The buck got up and disappeared over that rise!"

"Why didn't you shoot it again?" Jake asked. That was the next obvious question, and one I had no good answer for.

"I dunno," I muttered. "Figured the antelope had had it, and kept waiting for it to drop over dead. When we decided to shoot, Max's gun jammed."

Jake declared that he'd run up the slope and shoot it. Max was in no shape to finish the job, given his mental attitude as well as his physical condition. It would take him some time to climb up over the rise; it was time for quick action. He was now wringing his hands, blaming himself for this fiasco. I told him that this was just part of hunting and we'd get the buck. (I lied, this was something I'd never seen before. Wounded animals, yes, but none that got up and walked away as you were posing it for a picture.)

Jake ran up the slope and sneaked up to the crest. He looked down at us and pointed down to where we couldn't see. Then he gave the thumbs-up sign. I watched in relief as Jake laid down prone and took a rest. He was a good shot; I knew Max's antelope would finally be put down.

Jake fired, and again gave us the thumbs-up sign. Life was good.

When we reached the antelope, once more I asked Max to pose with it. He did, and I ran off a couple rolls of film. I noted a pretty lichen-covered rock a few yards away and asked Max to re-pose the antelope. I grabbed the buck's horn and began dragging it over to the rock when I noticed something amiss. There was no neck wound. This animal appeared to be hit once through the chest.

"Say, fellers," I said, "I dearly hope I'm wrong, but this might not be Max's antelope."

Both Jake and Max looked at me aghast, as though I'd committed a mortal sin.

"What'n hell you talkin' about?" Jake said.

"Yeah," quipped Max. "What'n hell you talkin' about?"

"Your buck had a big old hole in its neck, didn't it?" I asked Max.

Suddenly Max got the picture. Then it sunk in on Jake, too. Instantly both men jumped up and ran over to help me inspect the buck.

"Ain't no neck wound in this buck," I announced. "Everybody agreed?"

Silence.

"You got yourself a nice buck," I said to Jake. Get your tag out and let's get field-dressing. We'd best be hurrying too, because somewhere out there is Max's buck with a neck wound."

Not long afterward, we hiked over the top of the rise and I spotted a buck antelope running up a steep hillside alongside a fence. Every now and then the buck tried to jump the fence but it would fall back down. Antelope are terrible jumpers, anyway, and never try to leap fences. I've seen two do it in half a lifetime of observing and hunting antelope.

"That's got to be Max's buck!" I said. "It's stumbling around a lot. This time I'm going after it. I'll signal you guys from the top."

I sprinted after the buck. It was about 800 yards away, and by the time I huffed and puffed up the incline, it was gone. However, I found a spot of blood. It was indeed Max's long, lost antelope.

Reaching the top of the slope, I looked down to see an antelope laying in the sagebrush. I checked it with my binoculars. The animal was still, and I was sure it was dead.

It was about time. This whole escapade was beginning to wear thin. Max was beside himself with misery, and we all felt bad for the antelope. Now it was all over.

I signaled to Max and Jake, giving them the thumbs-up sign. They got in the truck to drive over and meet me at the dead antelope.

We got to the buck at the same time, and as I approached I saw something strange. This antelope was dead, all right, but it was tagged. Was I going nuts or was the sun taking its toll? I couldn't remember if Max had tied a tag to the buck, but didn't think he did so.

"I don't believe this," I said. "This antelope is tagged. Max, this ain't your buck! Then I saw the gutpile, which clinched it. I rolled the antelope a bit and saw that it had been fielddressed. Nope, it for sure wasn't Max's buck. Somebody else had shot the antelope, dressed and tagged it, and evidently went to get their vehicle.

Now we were frustrated big-time. Where in hell was Max's antelope?

We spent the rest of the morning looking, but no dice. Several dozen antelope were about, and we carefully checked out each buck with the spotting scope. None had a neck wound.

It's easy to spot the buck. Doe antelope have very small horns. The most aggressive bucks have the biggest harems.

A while later, we were sitting on a sunny hillside eating sandwiches when a buck walked out of the bottom and up onto the far side of the slope we were sitting on. It appeared to be healthy, moving along as any normal buck might.

Jake looked at it through the spotting scope, but didn't see anything out of the ordinary. Then he looked again.

"Take a look at this one," he said to me. "Am I seeing things, or does it look like his neck looks a little peculiar?"

After looking, I agreed with Jake. It seemed that there was a large spot of dirt on its neck. Jake and I decided that what we were looking at was dried blood.

The decision was made for Max to shoot this buck. The more we looked, the more we were convinced it was the one we'd chased so long.

Max fired and the buck went down. The three of us raced to the fallen animal, curious as hell as to what it was.

Hot damn! It was Max's buck, neck wound and all. We were overjoyed, and slapped each other on the back profusely. Max's first hunt was over, and I'm sure he'll never forget it. I won't either, and it taught me never to leave my gun in the truck again. To heck with that nonsense.

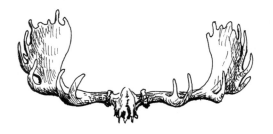

PASS THE HOT DOGS, THE TRUCK IS ON FIRE

Of all the hunts I've ever made, some stand out heads and shoulders above the others. Usually those memorable hunts have an element of danger, frustration, plain bad luck, or a combination of all three. This particular chapter recounts a hunt that I'll never forget. You'll understand why when you read it.

You might say that the flames that shot 30 feet out of Doug McKnight's truck were part of a bad dream, but they were painfully real. We watched helplessly as the vehicle burned furiously in the remote desert. There was nothing we could do; the nearest help was 70 miles away. I immediately said to heck with sheep hunting, because our options no longer existed. The flaming truck represented the end of the prized hunt.

"Too bad we don't have a few hot dogs," Doug said. "It's about time for lunch, and we've got a great barbeque fire goin'."

Doug's sense of humor at such a moment was typical, but I wasn't amused.

"You're a weirdo, ol' buddy," I responded. "Your truck is burning to the ground, and you're making jokes."

"Let's cry, then," he said, "or whine or pout. Fact of the matter is, ain't nothin' gonna save that truck, OR this hunt. We might's well save our sanity."

Actually, we tried to put the flames out when we first realized the truck was on fire. But, throwing sand and water on the burning undercarriage by lying down next to the truck didn't stop the flames. Moreover, our immediate thoughts were to unload the truck and move safely away, which is exactly what we did.

Doug was right about saving our sanity and trying to laugh, even a little bit. Any amount of mirth was no doubt therapeutic. We didn't need any more trauma.

The inferno engulfing the truck represented the end of a dream hunt. Against terrible odds, I'd drawn a desert bighorn sheep tag in Utah. As North American big game species go, the desert sheep is without a doubt the most elusive, and perhaps the most prestigious of all. Only two or three states offer desert sheep hunting, and getting a tag is akin to winning the Publisher's Weekly contest.

Up to now the hunt had been a disappointment. The season lasted 30 days; it would be over soon.

The day I learned I'd drawn the tag, my initial reaction was to gather up some good pals and have a proper celebration at the local Elks Lodge. When my head cleared a day or two later, I launched into researching the unit. A buddy had killed a ram there the year before, and he shared information, drawing an "X" on a map where he'd seen a number of good rams, including the one he killed.

"Piece of cake," Paul said about the hunt.

"Lead pipe cinch, really?" I asked. "No kidding?"

"Duck soup," he responded. "Easy hunt. Park the truck, walk a quarter mile and shoot a ram."

Paul, unfortunately, was not familiar with Zumboism, a term coined by my college classmates. It is the art of doing things wrong, with a great deal of help from Murphy.

I was accompanied on the first five days of the hunt by my good friend, the late Ken Heuser of Rifle, Colorado. Despite serious hip problems, Ken never complained once as we hiked 15 to 20 miles a day across rugged rocky rims in the southern Utah desert. The 100 plus degree heat didn't help.

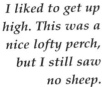

I liked to get up high. This was a nice lofty perch, but I still saw no sheep.

As good fortune would have it, or so I thought, we had inadvertently camped close to the only outfitter in the unit. He was a friendly chap, and offered suggestions as to where we might hunt. As the days passed and we saw no sheep, I began to suspect that perhaps the outfitter was purposely steering us away from the areas he was hunting with his client. On several occasions, however, we spotted them in the distance, hunting the same general area we were. When they returned to camp night after night without seeing sheep, as we did, I should have realized that this hunt might not go exactly as expected. The area my buddy had marked with an "X" hadn't held a sheep for months.

Ken and I never found a fresh track. It would have been wonderful to have spotted a ewe, or even a lamb, to indicate the presence of a sheep. Old droppings and weathered tracks were the only signs that sheep had ever been in the area.

The heat was unbearable. Ken and I left camp each day with

all the water we could comfortably carry, along with juicy fruits. I recall one occasion when the only liquid I had was in the form of a peach. The fruit was a special reward for getting through the afternoon, and I thought about it every 10 minutes and how luscious the juices would be.

The rattlesnake showed up when I was eating the peach. My brain was so numb from the heat, and I was so desperately involved with the delightful fruit, that I kicked at the snake that evidently hadn't seen my quiet form and was nonchalantly cruising on by. Ken watched from where he sat, with a look of astonishment on his face. The movement of my foot brought the rattler to immediate attention, and I was still unconcerned. Luckily the alarmed reptile crawled away, and as I sat around the campfire that night, I realized that the daytime temperatures were affecting my ability to reason. Any other time, that rattler would have instantly been dealt with in a rather violent fashion, and I wouldn't have been so complacent at its proximity to my foot. And to hell with snake lovers.

Ken and I were dog tired as we packed to leave after the fifth day of hunting. He needed to return to Colorado, and I intended to go home in northern Utah for a couple days, take care of some business, and immediately return to the sheep unit, spending the rest of the season there if necessary.

It didn't quite work out that way. On the drive home, news on the radio told about a Colorado outfitter who was attacked by a grizzly bear. While being terribly mauled by the furious bear, the outfitter managed to stab the bear with a hand-held arrow and kill it.

Being editor-at-large for OUTDOOR LIFE at the time, my duty was to be on the lookout for great stories. This was a great story, and my boss in New York agreed.

"Get to Colorado, quick," he said, "and get an exclusive on the grizzly attack. I want that story!"

Desert sheep hunting be damned, I thought unhappily, as I sped to the southern Colorado town where the badly injured outfitter was undergoing treatment in a hospital. I was not a happy camper.

Five days later, after being kicked out of the hospital many times by nurses who allowed me to talk to the outfitter only 20 minutes each day, I had my exclusive story. Time was running out on the sheep hunt, however, and it was a matter of putting the pedal to the metal, since it would take another couple days to get home, repack, and drive back down to the sheep unit. The state trooper, unfortunately, was completely disinterested in my excuse as he wrote the speeding ticket. What did he know about sheep hunting, anyway?

If sheep were in the canyon bottoms, it would take a hang glider or parachute to get to them.

Doug McKnight was eager to join me on the remainder of the hunt because he'd hunted the area before and was absolutely wild about sheep hunting. Ken had other commitments and couldn't make it.

Our first mistake was to park my truck at the rim of the desert and take Doug's truck down to the extremely rugged country where we'd hunt.

The term extremely rugged doesn't justly describe the terrain in the area. Far from it. Rocky outcrops jut up from the desert floor everywhere. Steep slickrock faces and topsy turvy ridges break up the landscape; what roads there are simply defy the imagination.

With Doug's truck loaded with our gear, we crept down the road, and at times I'd have to get out and direct Doug so the tires wouldn't slide us down to oblivion on narrow, twisting turns that were better suited for a mountain bike than a full-sized American-made pickup.

With a great deal of effort and resolve, we made it to the general area we wanted to camp, but we ran out of daylight. By the time we found the spot to pitch our tent, it was dark. Using the truck headlights to illuminate the area, we set up the tent, unloaded our gear, and called it a night.

Unfortunately we made a mistake, a very profound mistake. When Doug turned the key in the ignition to back the truck away from the tent, the battery was dead, thanks to us using the headlights without keeping the motor running.

A very dumb move on our part, but the error was done and couldn't be rectified. Our only option was to hike out to my truck and drive it in to camp. This was not a pleasant task, because my truck was at least 24 miles away, by our most conservative estimation.

Doug insisted that he walk out, because I could hunt sheep while he hiked and not lose a day of hunting. That seemed to be a good solution, but I was nonetheless feeling it was a bit unfair for Doug to make the walk. He'd have none of my arguments, however, and was adamant about walking out.

We came up with a guesstimate of how long it would take him to make the trip. A normal human being walks about three miles per hour at a brisk pace, but Doug is not a normal human being. He doesn't walk; he lopes. So figuring three and a half to four miles an hour, he should make it out in six to seven hours, and take another two hours or so to drive my truck in. Giving him an extra hour, a round trip of 10 hours should have done it. Therefore, if he left camp at six a.m., as was the plan, he should be back no later than four.

By four o'clock that afternoon I was about five miles from camp, looking for my first sheep track that wasn't five years old, or so they seemed. From a high vantage point I was able to see camp in the distance through my spotting scope, but no sign of Doug or my truck.

Before leaving that morning, I'd tossed an elk roast, some potatoes, onions, carrots, spices and water in a Dutch oven and buried it in hot coals. I was looking forward to a hearty dinner with Doug that evening, but thoughts of several icy drinks were foremost in my mind. The desert temperatures were still blow-torch hot, just as they were when I'd hunted with Ken. At 100 degrees plus, you think about liquids a lot. A whole lot.

It took me until dark to work my way back to camp. Still no sheep sign, and no Doug at camp. The worrying process was beginning.

As I sat around the campfire, with its flames lighting the dark-ness, my brain conjured all sorts of possibilities. Foremost was the prospect that Doug had suffered a bad migraine, and was unable to walk to the truck or drive it back in. He'd told me once that he'd had migraines so bad that he couldn't remember his name.

An hour or so later, I saw an eerie sight. The cliff face oppo-site camp seemed to suddenly glow in a bizarre light. As soon as it happened, it disappeared. Now then, I'm not totally posi-tive that UFO's don't exist, and I was so worked up from wor-rying about Doug that it didn't take much to get my imagination going in any direction.

Moments later another cliff was lit up by a light. Weird things were going on, and I'd often heard about UFO's using the remote Utah deserts as landing sites. I'd always dismissed those stories as hogwash, but now, sitting in the quiet, very dark desert with no human within a dozen or more miles, I began to wonder.

When the cliff walls took turns being bathed with lights, it suddenly occurred to me that the phenomenon was caused by the distant headlights of my truck as it weaved its way down the serpentine road.

Fifteen minutes later Doug drove up, with no good excuses for being so late other than he'd spotted some old sheep tracks while walking out and had spent a few hours checking some country higher up. Of course, I never let on that I was a nervous wreck. We ate well that night.

Three more days of intense hunting produced absolutely nothing. In prime spots we'd peer through spotting scopes for hours, but no sheep appeared. Spotting during the heat of the day is a standard way to hunt. It works if there are sheep around. If no sheep are present, you get a whole lot of eyestrain. Frustration is the order of the day.

It was time to go all out, to make a last ditch effort. Doug suggested we try a very remote spot that he was sure no sheep hunters had been to. It was about 25 miles from camp, and a treacherous road led to it. Once there, we intended to bivouac and live in the rocks, drinking water when we found it in tiny seeps, and eating dried food that we'd carry in our packs. No tent or sleeping bags; we'd sleep like animals, huddled in whatever sheltered places we could find.

The road was the worst I'd ever seen in a lifetime of hunting. It was a rocky passage that wound down the side of a mountain, built by uranium prospectors 40 years ago. To get down, I walked in front of Doug's truck and guided each tire off boulders as big as washtubs. We inched along, a few feet at a time, bouncing and lurching from one rock to the next.

Finally we made it to the desert floor, but within 10 minutes the truck was trapped in a blowsand wash. The sand was as fine as the type you see on a beach, and we were hopelessly mired. Trying to jack the truck up to put solid material under the tires didn't work either, because the sand was too deep, and the jack simply dug in under the truck's weight.

The jack needed to be on a solid base, but nothing was around. We hiked a quarter mile to some rocky ledges, but all we could find was sandstone which crumbled easily under the weight on the jack.

It suddenly occurred to us that the spare tire would make a perfect base. And it did. But jacking the truck up was just the beginning of the process. We still had to get something under the tires.

Three hours later the truck was free, but only after we'd turned it a full 180 degrees in the sand. We did this by jacking the front of the truck off the ground and pushing it off the jack. Little by little it nosed around, and we had it positioned where it could then be driven out.

Doug finally spun it away from the wash, but we were still on the wrong side. We had to attempt another crossing. Locating a better spot 50 yards up the wash, Doug got a head start, hit the wash and barreled across. At one point the truck was fully in the air, much as you'd see in a cops and robbers chase on TV.

With that major ordeal behind us, we walked over to a small juniper to eat a couple oranges. The tree offered the only shade around.

Suddenly Doug looked over at his truck and made a startling announcement.

"My truck's on fire!"

We ran as hard as we could and saw flames licking along the drive shaft and under the oil pan. Desperately we grabbed fistfuls of sand to throw on the flames, but we made no headway. Water from our jugs was no help either.

As the flames grew, we realized it was hopeless. Grabbing gear out of the cab, as well as our camp equipment in the pickup's bed, we made several quick trips hauling our possessions away from the burning vehicle. We had no idea why the truck caught fire. Our best guess was that we'd ruptured a fuel line when digging it out of the wash, and gas spilled on a hot surface and ignited.

With everything out of the truck, we stood back and watched helplessly. Deciding that our gear was still too close to the burning truck and expecting an explosion when the flames hit the two gas tanks, we carried everything we owned farther from the truck.

A few minutes later, a small brush fire developed, so we again moved our gear to another location devoid of vegetation. The brush fire was going nowhere. It would burn to a small ledge where the brush quit and go out on its own.

The explosions never came. Instead, the gasoline burned in a manner we hadn't expected. Twin torches of flame hissed out from each gas cap, much like an acetylene torch but much longer. Later I learned from firefighters that this was typical. Most vehicles that blow up are the work of Hollywood technicians. Nonetheless, the rest of the truck burned completely. Window glass was turned to liquid and dripped down, burning as it fell away.

When the inferno was at its peak, Doug remembered a handgun in the glove compartment that his grandfather had given him. It was a goner, along with other items behind the seat and in the glove box that we didn't have time to remove. Included in those items were dozens of rounds of ammo, some .22's and some high-powered cartridges. They exploded individually as the heat reached them, along with the truck battery, which made the most impressive blast of all.

Doug's truck burns to the ground...spelling the end of the truck and my sheep hunt.

It didn't take long before the truck was a pile of molten glass and metal. When it was over, Doug and I walked up to it, but we had nothing to say. I took a few photos of it for insurance purposes, since we doubted that any insurance claims agent would ever get back into that godforsaken place.

Speaking of that remote spot, we realized the next task at hand was to hike the 25 miles back to camp, and return in my truck to haul all the gear out that we'd salvaged from Doug's truck.

With two jugs of water we began the journey, starting at dark. Walking steadily, aided by starlight, we made it to camp sometime around two a.m. Being too wired to sleep, we broke camp immediately and by first light we were headed back to the remains of Doug's truck.

I wasn't looking forward to the journey, because my truck was brand new, and it was quite possible that the rock-studded road would seriously rearrange the looks of the rig.

It was slow going, as the truck bounced and slammed from one rock to another, each tire grabbing or sliding over whatever boulder that was under it.

Upon reaching the bottom, we made several long trips hauling our gear to my truck, because I wasn't at all willing to attempt crossing the blowsand wash. Murphy's law was still very much with us.

The sheep hunt was over. Although we could have given it a try the last couple days of the season, our spirits were broken. I admitted defeat.

That isn't exactly the end of this story, and it pains me to add this sequel. After we drove out of the desert, I learned that the outfitter I'd camped next to during the first week of the hunt had located two legal rams. His client shot one, and the other ran across a draw and laid down in full sight, watching the hunters dressing the other ram. The outfitter sent his guide to look for me, but, of course, I was gone. The guide found an empty camp.

I don't expect to ever draw a desert sheep tag in the U.S. again, and Mexico's sheep hunts are out of reach of my savings account. Nonetheless, the bittersweet memories of that Utah desert will remain with me forever. That, after all, is what hunting is really all about.

And never again will I say to heck with fire extinguishers. In each of my vehicles I now carry one.

A PACK RAT
HITCHES A RIDE

Though I'd hunted moose in Canada quite a bit, my first hunt in the U.S. was in Wyoming in the late 1970's. I was a Utah resident at the time, and had drawn a tag near the Utah border. That moose hunt was an eye-opener. Assuming the hunt would be a piece of cake, I failed to scout the area as thoroughly as I should have. More importantly, I didn't investigate the potential of the unit in terms of trophies. I figured, unfortunately, that big bulls would be available, and to get one I'd just hunt a little harder than other hunters in the unit. I soon learned that my assumption was dead wrong.

Prior to the hunt I'd obtained a map from the U.S. Forest Service office and located various areas that would be attractive to moose. Most often those were willow bottoms adjacent to dense stands of evergreen timber composed of douglas fir, lodgepole pine, spruce, and alpine fir.

When I did a bit of scouting a couple days before the season, I saw plenty of fresh sign in a big willow bottom, and I was satisfied. No other hunters were about, which was a welcome circumstance. I figured I had the place to myself.

Unfortunately, that wasn't the case when hunting season arrived. Opening morning didn't have plenty of hunters, certainly nothing compared to deer and elk seasons, but there were just enough people to keep things stirred up.

Because a forest road bisected the willow bottom, access was excellent, which accounted for a concentration of hunters. In retrospect, I should have taken the time to find a place off the beaten track; less likely to be visited by hunters. On the other hand, I had no horses to transport a moose out of the woods, so my plan was to stay as close to the road as possible, no more than a quarter mile away. That was apparently the intention of most other hunters, thus the competition.

Three bulls were killed by hunters on the first day; two of them were spotted from the road and dropped close by. The other was easily driven to. I was determined to make a hunt out of it, and spent most of my time away from the road and other hunters. My neighbor, Alan Massey, accompanied me on the hunt. Alan is great company, and a strong guy. It's good to have a strong guy along on a moose hunt.

I didn't see a moose the first day of the season, but I wasn't too concerned. Sooner or later I'd spot a good bull, or so I thought. After all, moose were supposed to be fairly easy to find, and hunters normally have a very high success rate.

It was on the afternoon of the second day when I jumped the bull out of a clump of firs. He wasn't a big bull, but had an antler spread of about 30 inches. He flushed 20 yards away, and I had plenty of time for a fairly easy shot as he ran toward the forest from his hiding spot at the edge of the trees.

I opted not to shoot, believing I could do better. Watching him increase the gap between us, I almost changed my mind, but decided to let him go.

Nothing but a spike bull and two cows showed up the next two days, but I still wasn't worried. The season ran for a month, and I had another week within that framework to hunt.

Alan and I drove into town to pick up supplies, and ran into

These are typical bulls in the unit. Not much antler,
but plenty of meat!

an old friend who worked for the U.S. Forest Service. When I told him I was moose hunting, and passed up the 30 inch bull, he was obviously surprised.

The man allowed as to how I hadn't done my homework. If I had, he stated, I'd have taken the bull with no hesitation. It seemed that the biggest bulls in the unit were sporting antlers not much wider than 24 inches.

I saw a game warden at a store a bit later, and he confirmed the bad news. Because the unit doesn't have a great deal of cover and good access is available, bulls don't tend to live long. Most hunters took the first bulls they saw.

We went home after hunting a couple days more. My efforts were in vain; I didn't see a single bull, even a spike. Though I hunted intently the area where I'd seen the 30-inch bull, he'd disappeared.

While getting my camp trailer ready to leave, we discovered

that a pack rat had somehow gotten inside and made itself quite at home in one of the cabinets. I remembered hearing strange sounds in the night, and thought there were critters outside. We couldn't locate the rat, but heard it squeaking every now and then as we pounded on the walls. The son of a gun was intent on riding home with us.

The trip home was in the midst of one of those blizzards you'd like to forget about, but can't. It was nearly a white-out situation, and at times I stopped smack in the middle of the highway because I couldn't see a thing, not even the hood ornament of my pickup. It didn't help matters that it was dark, but I doubt if we could have seen much even in the daytime.

As we crawled along, I figured we should be pretty close to a town. I was guiding myself by watching the reflectors along the road that appeared every now and then in my headlights. Nothing else was identifiable.

"I wonder where in hell that town is?" I said to Alan.

After a few moments of silence, he answered. "I think we're in it," he said. "What's that funny light up there in the sky?"

A gas station -- that's what it was. The light was the sign, and we'd been in town for four blocks and didn't know it. We holed up in a cafe that we knew was across from the gas station and waited out the storm. The pack rat, by the way, was never seen nor heard from again. He got out when the gettin' was good, and obviously said to heck with living in camp trailers.

When I returned to the unit a couple weeks later, I found the area much more to my liking. Ten inches of snow covered the ground, allowing tracking opportunities, provided, of course, I could find a moose track in the first place. To my delight, no other hunters were around.

After hiking through the snow for three hours, I located two sets of tracks. Both appeared to be the same size, and I had an idea that a big cow and a young bull were traveling together. I'd made up my mind to take the first bull to show up. If the area held no respectable bulls, it was obviously a waste of time to look for anything decent, especially since a good share of the moose were already taken by hunters. Since I was a nonresident of Wyoming at the time, I had a bull-only license. Residents were allowed to take an animal of either sex in that unit.

I glass for moose while following three-day old tracks in the snow. Tracking moose is great fun.

The tracks were very old, perhaps made three days earlier. They represented a special challenge, and I took off after them immediately. Now then, it appears to be a rather simple exercise to track a pair of moose in the snow, and I'm sure it would be if they were lined out or at least going in one general direction. These moose, however, fed extensively in small areas, leaving tracks going in every direction. Worse yet, a light powder of fresh snow covered the tracks just enough so it was hard to tell which direction they were going. It didn't matter much anyway, because they left a maze of tracks as they walked in circles and figure eights.

My only option was to find where the tracks left the willows for the forest. At one point I thought I'd located their exit route, but the tracks went up a sagebrush slope, turned, and headed back down into the willows.

Another set of tracks that departed the willows proved to be correct. I followed, and found where the moose had bedded under a large spruce tree. When the tracks left that spot, I knew I'd gained a day on the animals. Their beds represented a day-time rest area where they'd spent eight or ten hours.

And so it went. I continued to sort out the puzzle, hitting stumbling blocks more often than not. Eventually I figured them out, and by so doing, I ultimately worked through the confusing trail.

Soon I found a second bedding spot, and I knew I was getting close. The tracks were much crisper and sharper than they'd been when I first took up the trail.

Presently I heard a swishing sound in the brush. I couldn't see what it was, but I believed I'd flushed the moose. Their tracks proved me correct. Great gouges were etched into the snow where the fleeing moose bolted through the vegetation.

I quickly moved up to where I'd heard the sound and saw that the moose had split up. Since both tracks were almost equal in size, I chose one and hoped I was trailing a bull.

Fifteen minutes later, I realized that my quarry was the wrong sex. A big cow appeared in the brush, and immediately scooted off when she spotted me.

So much for my moose hunt. Darkness was a few minutes away, and with it the close of the season. I had no choice but to say to heck with the moose hunt. The next time I hunted a moose, I'd be much more familiar with the place I hunted and the individual animals within it.

Since moose have a relatively small home range, they have a tendency to live in the same tiny area for long periods of time. It's not uncommon for a moose to be seen in the same timbered basin or willow thicket for weeks. That being the case, hunters who have done some looking prior to the season normally score because they've already pinpointed the quarry.

A few years ago, a buddy drew a moose tag in a forested area in northwest Wyoming. I'd seen a very good bull several times while fishing for brookies in the summer, and told my friend exactly where the moose was living.

I accompanied my pal on the hunt, and as we scouted prior to the opener, we found the moose within 300 yards of where I'd been seeing him that summer. Luckily, no other hunters spotted him; my pal collected him nicely on opening morning. If it was I who had the tag, Murphy's Law no doubt would have prevailed and the bull would have mysteriously vanished. Moose hunting just doesn't agree with me, as I learned after hunting moose in Canada and the West. I'm still looking for a really good bull.

During the rut, which occurs in September and October, bull moose tend to be wanderers, traveling about as they seek females. They'll move all day long until they find an unaccompanied cow. If the cow has a bull with her, the challenger may run him off, or be run off himself. Frequently they'll have a go at each other, sparring fiercely. That's what I witnessed in British Columbia during a moose hunt, which is recounted in another chapter. And did I get a big bull on that trip? I'll make you read about it to find out.

A good strategy is to get up as high as possible, looking for traveling moose. A unique aspect during the rut is the fact that moose move all day long; you can see them anytime.

Normally, moose are seldom active during the daylight. They're similar to elk and deer in that they feed throughout the night, early in the morning and late in the afternoon. They'll typically be bedded within an hour or two after sunrise.

It's amazing how moose can conceal themselves, even in low willows. They can easily bed out of sight by day, appearing as if by magic by late afternoon. For that reason, you must be persistent. Just because you don't see them right off doesn't mean they're gone. Moose are big, and fairly easy to see in the open, but when feeding in tall brush or bedded they might be totally concealed by vegetation.

There's an area in Yellowstone Park that never fails to hold moose. It's a long strip of willows along a stream bordered by a highway. A sign that says "look for moose" invites tourists to stop. You can drive by that wet area all day long and look until your eyes blur, and never see a moose. But give it a try the first couple hours of light and the last hour of the afternoon and you'll see three to five moose almost without fail.

Some years ago, while heading to the high country to cut a load of firewood, I saw a big bull at the edge of willows near a thick stand of lodgepole pine. He had a unique rack that was thin and wide.

The Shiras moose of the Rockies is quite at home in the forest. I've seen them in timber at 10,000 feet.

I told my neighbor about the bull. When he went up for a load of firewood a week later he saw the bull 50 yards from where I'd spotted him.

Word got around about the bull, and before long several people began looking for him. Almost everyone saw him in that same spot, but always early in the morning or late in the afternoon.

When moose tags were assigned for that unit in the lottery draw, one of the lucky hunters called and asked me about the moose. He hadn't seen it, but had heard about it from someone else. I pinpointed the spot exactly, but the hunter never saw the moose on the opener. The bull went unseen for the rest of the season, and seemed to have disappeared. I had no idea what had happened to the moose; he was simply too visible and trusting. He probably wandered off somewhere, looking for a tastier patch of fresh willows. Some of my bad luck might have rubbed off on that poor guy.

During deer season I went up past the spot, and there was the bull, bigger than life, eating willow twigs within five yards of the first spot I'd seen him in late summer. Where that moose had gone I'll never know, but he'd found another place he liked. I doubt he was smart enough to hide; he probably headed to another feeding area and simply went undiscovered. Maybe he said to heck with that hunting area just before the season started. One thing I don't care for much is a smart moose.

Not many folks get to hunt moose in the Rockies, but there's plenty of reason to try for them. They're big, unique, and excellent eating. Many people rank them at the very top of the list of best-tasting big game. When you get a moose, you get a LOT of moose. You'll have plenty of memories, too. And remember, the best moose, in the minds of most hunters, is the one that falls closest to the road. Keep that in mind when you're looking for the big one, and don't be surprised if he pulls a disappearing act. Moose have a way of doing exactly that. Ask me. I can tell you all about it.

DO I HAVE TO CROSS THAT RIVER?

Dall sheep country. It is a wild, high region, where you feel close to the Almighty and the world is in perspective. The Dall's domain is a magnificent piece of land, sometimes appearing lonely, but never empty. Only one region in the world – Alaska and the Yukon, are home to Dall sheep.

To many, a wild sheep is the ultimate prize in all of North American hunting. This is the animal that builds fantasies among mortals, whether they intend to hunt them or not. A sheep is to a hunter as a morel is to a mushroom gatherer; a super bowl ring to a football player. Sheep hunting is the quintessence of our sport. No big game animal in the continent rates a higher rank.

93

I've had the good fortune of hunting sheep a number of times, and I will remember every hour of every hunt. Nothing will dim those impressions, those treasured moments that are among my favorite memories.

I can blame the late Jack O'Connor for my attraction to sheep and sheep country. I read his stories with fervor, experiencing his hunts vicariously. I could almost feel the chilled mountain air, smell the wildflowers, taste the sweet water of high-country creeks, and see the great rams in the lofty peaks.

Because of his articles, I regarded sheep hunting as the ultimate pursuit of all big game hunting. When other kids were thinking about hot rods and girls, I was dreaming of climbing high peaks and eating sheep ribs around a campfire. But at the time I was just a kid growing up in New York State. Sheep hunting was only a silly dream.

In reality I had cottontail rabbits, squirrels, ruffed grouse, and whitetail deer to look forward to. I had no illusions that someday I might hunt a sheep.

My life took an unexpected turn, and I moved west before I was 20 to study forestry and wildlife. All the animals that I'd read about – elk, mule deer, antelope, cougars, and others, became common quarry. I hunted every chance I could, taking vacation time from my job as a forest ranger to guide for outfitters, and to trek new mountain ranges on weekends. I couldn't get enough of the West.

Those thoughts went through my mind as I looked down at the Alaskan Highway from the Cessna, flying toward my first Dall sheep hunt in the Wrangell Mountains.

The Wrangells. The name rolls off the tongue easily, commanding respect and awe. These are not among the largest mountain ranges on earth, but are among the grandest. Students of geology and trivia know that this extremely rugged range lies in Alaska, close to the Yukon border. Hunters, however, know the Wrangells as prime game country, offering grizzlies, moose, goats, caribou, and Dall sheep.

As we flew, I wondered if this hunt would equal the excitement and hazards of some other sheep hunts.

A desert sheep hunt in Utah in 1980 almost resulted in tragedy when my pal's pick-up truck caught fire and burned furiously, turning it into a heap of molten metal and glass. Just before the fire, the truck was hopelessly stuck in blowsand, and my friend and I worked several hours to get it out. While doing so, we apparently damaged the fuel line, allowing gasoline to come in contact with the engine block. Luckily, we were not injured, and had to walk 24 miles across a searing hot 110-degree desert without water. Of 17 sheep hunters that year, only two killed rams. I was not among the successful pair. Unfortunately, I said to heck with that desert sheep hunt before the hunt was over. Elsewhere in this book I give the full account of that hunt.

In 1986, I hunted Rocky Mountain bighorn sheep near my home in Cody, Wyoming. The remote area we hunted, just outside Yellowstone Park, is a favorite place for wildlife officials to drop "bad" grizzlies that continually cause problems around campgrounds and cabins, or were considered dangerous. Some of those temperamental bears raided our camp regularly, causing me to hasten my sheep hunting efforts. I took a ram, but only after a number of wide-awake nights when grizzlies roamed about. My magnum rifle was of little consolation. Unless the bear is chewing on you, or you can smell his stinking breath as he charges, killing a grizzly in Wyoming will result in a serious bout with the law. You can read about that hunt in another chapter.

Now, heading for the Dall sheep hunt, the pilot turned the airplane into a canyon, and we left the valley that we'd been following. Mountain walls seemed to be just yards from each wing, but I knew there was a safe air cushion between the Cessna and the steep slopes.

Although I've been to Alaska many times, it never gets old. The splendor of the vast land is never lost. It has a magical quality about it, a charisma that excites me every time I go there.

I will never forget my first trip to Alaska many years ago, and my feelings when the jetliner settled to the runway in Anchorage. Seeing this fabled land for the first time was an emotional high, and I felt as though my life was complete. Every new place afterward would be anticlimactic.

The Wrangells appeared more rugged than I expected. Enormous glaciers forever sealed the canyons and draws in the upper reaches, where jagged spires and peaks reached high into the sky. The highest elevations were gray rock walls and abrupt cliffs, interrupted by scree slopes zippered here and there into the mountain landscape. Green basins and benches were scattered about, offering forage to the big game animals that dwelled in the precarious terrain.

This was to be an interesting hunt in many ways. After my jetliner landed at the Fairbanks airport, I walked outside to catch a cab to the hotel I was to stay at. At the curb I spotted a young blonde woman who also was waiting for a cab. Her baggage included what seemed to be a gun case, identical to mine.

"Is that a gun case?" I asked dumbly.

"Yes it is," she answered.

"You're going hunting?" I questioned, with a bit of disbelief in my voice.

"Yes," was the simple reply.

"What are you hunting?" was my next inquiry.

"Dall sheep," she said.

"With who?" I asked, now with a great deal of interest.

"Terry Overly," she replied.

I was amazed. This attractive woman was going on an Alaskan sheep hunt by herself, and was to be on the same hunt with me. As I soon learned, Joann was a no-nonsense, hard hunter who worked every bit as hard as the rest of the hunters in our camp. She never complained once about any discomforts, and was great company on the hunt. We shared a cab to the hotel, met other hunters in our party, and talked excitedly about the upcoming adventure.

The next day, our small plane landed on the dirt strip after a long ride, and we were greeted by our outfitters, Terry and Debbie Overly. We were shown to the lodge area, which is a series of lovely log buildings. Some of the buildings are reserved for hunters, another is home to Terry and Debbie. A fine meal prepared by a talented cook completed the evening, and I wandered about a bit after dinner, taking in the local sights.

The following morning I rode horseback with the rest of our hunting party, headed for spike camp in good sheep country. The leader of our group was not what you'd expect in this rugged land. Instead of the typical broad-shouldered, leather-skinned outfitter that you'd find in most backcountry hunting camps, we were being guided by Debbie, who stood barely five feet tall, weighing in at 95 pounds.

We rode horseback from camp every day to get into sheep country. Then it was a matter of hiking up very rocky, steep slopes to get to the rams.

Debbie Overly is the sort of woman that feature writers are searching for. Hers is a fascinating story, certainly a departure from the average urban American female. Her lifestyle is even more amazing when considering her upbringing in southern California. You might understand her transition to the Alaska wilds if she was raised on a ranch in Montana, or a farm in Nebraska. But here she was, riding her favorite horse, guiding our pack train 12 miles from base camp to a lonely hunting area.

Debbie is a registered Alaskan guide, living full-time in the bush with her husband Terry. Together they run one of the finest sheep camps in North America.

Debbie and Terry Overly look over some sheep on a rugged mountainside.

Terry is a legend in his own right, and is easily spotted in a crowd. Look for a tall man with the looks of Clint Eastwood, jet black hair that seems a trifle too long, wearing a black Stetson, black shirt, and black trousers and you'll be looking at Terry. But before you evaluate him, spend a few days with him in the outback, and fly with him in his famous jet-black Super-Cub. Only then you'll know him for what he is, a top-rate outdoorsman who will always be a survivor. They don't come much tougher.

The campfire burned vigorously as our small party sat on stumps and spinned yarns of past hunts. My tentmate, Joe Moore, of Butte, Montana, shared his excitement with the rest of us. This was his first Alaskan sheep hunt, a dream long in the making. Like me, Joe was not looking for a trophy ram, but a nice, representative animal. And, like me again, the mystique of merely being on an Alaskan sheep hunt was as important as the kill, perhaps of greater importance. Joann was also on her first Dall sheep hunt, and was as full of anticipation as the rest of us.

Night was not far off when the drone of the airplane merged with the sounds of the nearby stream. Without looking up, Debbie announced Terry's imminent arrival.

Moments later the black aircraft bounced along the gravel of the uneven riverbottom and slowed to a stop just 25 yards from camp. Terry lashed the Super-Cub securely and soon joined us around the fire. He would hunt with us for two days, then he'd leave and ferry hunters, supplies, and sheep back to base camp.

"How many hunters do you think will score?" I asked as we watched the glowing red embers.

"All 11 of them," he said simply.

His answer was not egotistical, and there was no trace of bragging. It was an honest statement.

"There are lots of sheep in this country," Terry said. "You'll see rams every day, because our spike camps are located in the very best areas. I make sure the rams aren't overharvested in any spot, and take only one or two sheep each year from a major drainage that might encompass hundreds of square miles."

The idea of seeing rams each day was intriguing, setting this hunt apart from a multitude of others. There aren't many places, or big game species, that offer a consistent look at the quarry. I was eager for the hunt to start in the morning.

Because it was mid-August, the days were long and the nights short. The sun rose very early in the morning, but we weren't required to get up before sunrise, as in most other big-game hunts. Therein lay the basic strategy of hunting mountain sheep.

One of the hunters crosses a muddy river that had deep holes.

Terry explained the plan for the day as we ate a leisurely breakfast. Hunting early in the morning seldom worked because sheep were still feeding in the lower elevations. Because of the openness of the country and the sheep's sharp eyesight, we were apt to be spotted as we rode up the bottoms of the drainages, spooking the foraging animals out of the country. If, however, the sheep were bedded high on the slopes, they'd watch us intently, allowing us to ride by. We'd be able to evaluate the rams from a distance and plan a stalk.

As I learned the first morning, a stalk isn't always possible. We'd spotted nine rams bedded under a cliff. They eyed us cautiously, but seemed relaxed, almost as if they knew we couldn't approach. Because of the cliff, we wouldn't be able to get within a quarter mile of the rams.

Through the spotting scope, we saw that one of the sheep was a good animal. He had full curl horns, which is minimum for Dalls in the Wrangells, and his horns seemed heavy with a wide flare.

Terry and Debbie decided that the sheep was worth waiting for, so we spent the afternoon watching them. I was impatient, even though I knew it would be futile to try a stalk. I would have been willing to somehow try an impossible approach, but that would have been foolish and dangerous.

I forced myself to sit tight in the gravel of a glacial moraine. With luck, the rams would soon head down to green vegetation to feed. We were well out of sight, and by the relaxed attitude of the sheep, they apparently had forgotten about our presence earlier in the day.

The plan almost worked. About an hour before dark, the herd of bedded rams got to their feet and slowly meandered down the slope. Soon they were in the creek bottom, out of sight.

Terry and I were just about to move but the biggest ram suddenly reappeared, trotted up the mountain, and laid down in almost the exact place he'd been bedded all afternoon.

We couldn't figure it out. There was no wind change, we hadn't made a sound, but somehow the ram was uncomfortable in the bottom.

We watched as several of the other rams fed within 50 yards of our location. Finally we backed off and rode back to camp. Darkness was quickly approaching, and the big ram apparently had no intentions to move.

On the way back, a curious caribou approached and followed us most of the way to camp. He was quite bold, following only 50 yards behind us. Terry told us that the animal had no fear because we were undoubtedly the first humans it had ever seen.

The ride back to camp each night was most interesting,

almost enough for me to say to heck with Dall sheep hunting. On the way out each morning, our horses easily waded creeks that were about a foot deep. During the day, however, the hot sun melted the glaciers and the creeks were quickly transformed into ominous rivers that ran swift and very deep. Because the water was colored like chocolate milk, we couldn't see bottom and had no idea where the deep spots were. By sheer experience, Terry rode along the river and selected a safe crossing site.

Debbie Overly and I pose with my Dall ram.

How he did it I'll never know. What we didn't want was for the horses to step into a six-foot or deeper hole. In that rushing, frigid river, the results could have been tragic.

Thanks to Terry's skills (and later Debbie's — after Terry left our hunting party), we crossed the rivers without incident each night, but, at least in my case, not without a whole lot of misgivings and apprehension. The trick was to point the horse's head upstream by reining hard, and not allowing the animal to face downstream where the current could upend it, and the rider as well. At all times the horse had to be controlled so it was wading slightly upsteam as it crossed. Luckily we had to endure the high-water crossings only in the evening, because the glaciers quit melting during the cool nights and the streams receded to mere creeks.

Three days later, after looking at and turning down many rams, we hiked up a steep slope and found what we were looking for. Debbie had spotted a bunch of sheep on a mountainside, and we eased our way up, using a small, rocky creek as a route.

When we gained the elevation we wanted, we suddenly discovered a small ram looking at us. He stared for what seemed like hours, but it was probably 15 minutes; then he slowly moved around the bend.

Presently, more rams appeared, including one that had respectable horns. Joann was with us on the stalk and had opted to pass on the ram. I think, however, she was deferring to me because I had only another day to hunt and she had the better part of a week. (As it turned out, the gracious lady took a very fine ram a couple days later.)

When the unsuspecting ram walked well within range, my .30/06 bullet claimed him nicely.

He was a fine animal, with full-curl horns that measured 36 inches. By dark we had him to the horses, and we were in camp after a two-hour ride.

The campfire had a very special glow that night. Joe Moore also killed a sheep, and we toasted the brace of rams as firelight reflected off nearby spruces.

It had been one of those hunts that seemed to evolve perfectly. Except for the swollen streams that required care in crossing, our adventure had offered no extraordinary dangers.

That's not to say, however, that it was not etched forever in my brain. Fresh grizzly tracks in the sand, trusting caribou that allowed us to approach closely; bald eagles wheeling across Alaskan skies – all those special memories were a part of the Wrangell Mountains.

And that's what sheep hunting is all about. Now I understand why Jack O'Connor loved to hunt sheep more than anything else. His evaluation of sheep ribs roasted over a fire was right on the mark, too. It just doesn't get any better.

I'LL NEVER CLIMB
THAT MOUNTAIN AGAIN

Goat Rocks

If you asked me to describe the toughest physical hunt I've ever been on, I won't hesitate to answer. I'm talking about a technical challenge here, one that required strength, stamina, and possibly above all, a no-fear attitude. I'm not referring to long-term endurance – many elk hunts come to mind. The big-time challenge was on a goat hunt in Montana.

I'd drawn a goat tag in 1984, and was eager to go as soon as the season started on September 1. Bruce Scott, an outfitter friend who lives in the Bitterroot Valley, suggested I wait a while, because the goat pelt wouldn't be prime. A November goat, he explained, would be gorgeous, with long, thick fur and beautiful pantaloons (the long hair that goes down to the knees).

Bruce, in fact, volunteered to go along and provide the camp and horses if I'd wait, since he had elk hunters to take earlier. My hunt was in the Bitterroot Mountains, just a dozen miles from Bruce's home.

It wasn't a tough decision. I decided to wait. This was my first goat hunt, and I wanted to make the most of the hunt as well as having a pretty trophy for the wall. I knew that a November hunt would be far more difficult, because it was likely that we'd have to deal with snow and ice on very steep mountain slopes, along with plenty of goat rocks. The term "goat rocks" should be taken seriously if anyone tells you that you'll be hunting in them. Goat rocks are awful busted, jumbled mountaintops that seem to defy walking, climbing – anything but sophisticated rock climbing gear. But that's where goats often live, and that's where you hunt if you want a goat. Add some ice to those rocks, and you have a most perilous situation, making you want to say to heck with goat hunting.

Another negative of a late hunt is the difficulty of seeing goats. Obviously, it's a heck of a lot easier to spot a white animal against a bare background, rather than one covered with snow. In September, goats stand out like moose on a golf course. There's hardly any missing them, unless the goat is bedded in a basin. Sooner or later, however, you'll spot goats if they're around and you look hard enough.

Joining our party was Bill Thomas, an information officer for the Montana Department of Fish, Wildlife and Parks in Missoula. Bill had an elk tag, and would wander around looking for an elk while Bruce and I searched for a goat.

True to form, there was plenty of snow and ice in the mountains when I arrived for the hunt. We rode horseback to camp, getting there just before nightfall. Bruce had a wall tent set up, complete with a most welcome wood stove as well as a supply of firewood.

It didn't take long to find a goat the next day. Actually we saw three. Bruce thought one was a billy and the other two nannies. It's often difficult to tell the two apart, because both have long horns, but the nannies tend to have thinner horns, whereas a billy's horns are wider at the base. Then too, the goat we thought was a billy was also dirty and had a stained yellow

Bruce and I evaluate a goat high up on the slopes.

belly. According to Bruce, that was a giveaway of a male, since they get themselves messy during the rut. Nannies stay pretty.

A goat with nine-inch horns is respectable anywhere, and you'll tell your grandkids about a 10-incher. This billy appeared to have nine inchers, so we decided to give him a try. Only one little obstacle in the way – a huge damned mountain that had incredibly steep slopes and an inch of ice on the rocks – goat rocks.

"Are we really going up there?" I said to Bruce, almost hoping he'd change his mind.

"No problem," he said in his usual jovial fashion. "It's not as bad as it looks. Just follow me."

Not as bad as it looks? It looked almost straight up to me. But what the heck, if this was what it took to get a goat, then I was ready to go. Though I was admittedly a bit intimidated by the looming icy walls.

The first part of the journey was a piece of cake. We climbed up through a forest, and though we had to negotiate some serious timber, blowdowns, and other tangles, at least we had good footing on the forest floor. It was the rest of the climb that would be dangerous.

When we broke out of the timber, Bruce hiked upward, always setting his boots down on a skinny crack that held some soil. I'm talking skinny here – the crack was two inches wide. It was absolutely the only foothold; everything else was ice. There I was, tightroping that crack, and using fingers to balance myself. It was not my idea of a good time.

Slowly we gained elevation, and miracle of miracles, we were fairly close to where we'd seen the goats, though they were out of sight. Suddenly we saw two goats running along a rocky escarpment, and I figured we were done. Scratch this climb.

"I think those were the nannies," Bruce whispered. "Maybe the billy is still around."

Maybe. And maybe I'd hit the 10 million dollar lottery in the morning.

Just then I saw a funny look on Bruce's face. He was pointing directly behind me. Slowly I turned to see the billy staring at us.

I'll never forget the sight of that goat as he stood on the rim of a cliff that fell away to oblivion. The animal was only 75 yards away, and he was on my wish list, but there was a tiny problem. If he fell off the cliff, we might never reach him if he got caught in one of the many precipices below us. That's happened to many unfortunate goat hunters. A properly hit goat could, and sometimes does, fall away into a place where it cannot be reached by humans. The only thing that can get to it is a raven or eagle.

But there was a possible solution. Directly below the goat

grew a bush. If I could drop him in his tracks the bush would catch him and we could get to the goat. Big if. Even a heart or lung-shot animal will run some distance before succumbing. The only way I could pull this off would be to hit him in the spine.

Another problem. A goat has a unique anatomy. He has a big, deep chest as well as plenty of long, thick hair. I could probably spine-shoot a deer or elk at that range, but I wasn't sure of the goat's skeletal makeup.

"What if the goat falls below?" I whispered to Bruce. I wanted to know my options.

"I'd say there was a good chance we could get to it, but it might take all day," he responded.

I decided to shoot, and mentally traced where I thought his spine would be. At that close range, I should have been able to hit a golf ball. My .30/06 was nestled solidly in a notch in the rocks, pillowed by my hat.

I must have been living right that week. The bullet struck the goat in the spine, and he collapsed in the bush. I was dumbfounded that the plan had worked, expecting instead a long trek down the mountain and back up to get the goat.

He was a dandy billy, with nine-inch horns. His pelt was luxurious, thick and very long, but badly yellowed from urine and stained with mud.

"Don't worry about how he looks now," Bruce said. "Your taxidermist will whiten him up perfectly."

Now we had the job of getting the animal down. After field-dressing the goat, Bruce offered to go back down the mountain and get the packframes while I boned the meat. I thought that was a great idea. Once off this mountain I had absolutely no intentions of climbing back up.

I was boning away when I heard a voice behind me. "You don't have to take that meat," Bill Thomas said. "Even with our strict meat-waste laws, you can leave that for the ravens."

Bill was referring to the strip of meat below the knee down to the shin. It was mostly muscle and tissue, but I always use it, cooking it up in a stew pot and making it fork-tender. He was right. Most people discard those strips, but I'm known among my family and friends to be the consummate carcass cleaner.

Nothing goes to waste.

"What the heck are you doing up here?" I said. "No elk down below?" I was amazed to see that Bill had made the climb.

"Just curious to see what you got. Nice goat," Bill said. "That's one of the better ones."

Coming from Bill, who works for the game department, I was right proud of myself.

I pose with my mountain goat on the icy mountainside.

Bill went on to look for elk, and soon Bruce appeared with a packframe and rucksack. We'd lash the head and cape on the frame, and I'd put the meat in the rucksack. Though I didn't leave behind an ounce of meat, I was surprised at how little was on the carcass. As I recall, I got about 70 pounds of boned meat. Evidently a goat looks big because of its long fur and big skeletal frame.

The descent down the mountain was even more dicey. It was

difficult trying to keep our balance with heavy loads on our backs. I can tell you I was mighty happy to feel pine needles under my feet when we reached the edge of the forest.

When I got home, some friends told me it was impossible to make anything edible out of some of the tough meat I salvaged. I was determined to make them eat their words, along with some of the meat.

I filled a heavy pot with chunks of the meat along with onions, celery, chicken broth and seasonings, and set it atop my woodstove at sunup. Several hours later I added potatoes, carrots, more spices, and by sundown the stew was ready to eat. It was so tender a knife was a waste of time. My buddies apologized, but only after they'd had seconds and thirds. While enjoying the goat, I almost forgot about the miserable journey up and down that treacherous mountain. Almost, but not quite.

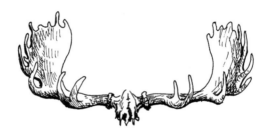

THE MOOSE
THAT CAME TO CAMP

Jim Treacy looked out the front door of the cabin and gasped, but I wasn't aware of anything wrong.

When he uttered, "My God, there's a moose!" I bolted from the table and looked over his shoulder. I was astounded. A bull moose was cautiously making his way through the timber no more than a football field away from the cabin.

Wilfred Ryan and his guides banged their cups of tea on the table and dashed over to the door. When they saw the moose, they glanced at each other in disbelief.

"A gun," I whispered loudly, "somebody get me a gun. I'll try to head him off and get a shot." The reaction in the cabin was one of complete pandemonium.

The adventure began several months before, when Jim and I decided that a moose hunt would be the ultimate adventure for our modest budgets. After talking about moose hunting for years, we agreed to finally do it.

The first problem we faced was to find an outfitter. A friend of ours had recently returned from Newfoundland with a fine bull. He hunted with Wilfred Ryan and recommended him highly. Jim wrote to Wilfred and learned that the last week of the fall moose season was available. We took it without hesitation, and added three more to our party. Jack Karnig, Bob Keegan, and Mailler "Fergie" Ferguson, rounded out our party of five.

Moose camp -- but a very WET moose camp.

This was to be my first-ever outfitted hunting trip. Little did I know that my career would lead me to dozens of outfitted trips in the future. History was in the making, at least for me, personally.

Out in the stormy north Atlantic ocean, this big ferry pitched like a cork. I should have brought motion-sickness pills.

When the long awaited time of departure finally arrived, we loaded two pick-up trucks that would take us on the long drive north. Fergie's pick-up was loaded with most of the gear, since it was hoped that my truck would soon be laden with moose meat.

The first several hundred miles were uneventful, but a thick fog blanketed New Brunswick and made driving a nightmare. We were thankful that we had allowed plenty of time to get to North Sydney, Nova Scotia, where we would board the ferry for the ride to Newfoundland. Being a very large island off the coast of Nova Scotia, you don't get to it unless you fly or float. We floated – big mistake. This was to be a journey we'd never forget.

Any enthusiastic thoughts we had about the finale of the trip were quickly dispelled by a radio announcement. The hurricane we had vaguely heard about several days before was now sweeping toward the Maritime Provinces. It would hit full force that afternoon.

Our spirits were dampened, but we didn't give up hope as we drove toward North Sydney. Our arrival there was greeted by powerful winds that lashed the trucks and sent huge waves crashing into piers and buildings. We parked at the ferry landing area and learned that the big ship was heaving too badly to be loaded. We would have to wait until the seas calmed a bit before boarding.

Finally, after a six hour wait, we were allowed to board. It didn't seem to me that the ship was heaving any less violently than before, but we clambered aboard anyway.

After the trucks were loaded, the ferry crew carefully secured each vehicle. It quickly became obvious why the trucks were tied down so well. As soon as we steamed out of the harbor, we were buffeted by monstrous waves that appeared to be over 30 feet high. It was impossible to stand upright without firmly holding on to a piece of the ship.

Our original intentions were to spend the journey in the cocktail lounge which was on the third story of the ferry. We figured to play cards and relax from the long drive. All of us were too keyed up to sleep.

It didn't take long to change our minds. The seas were so rough that the huge ferry rolled and pitched violently, rising and falling in the unbelievably deep swells. When the ship was at the bottom of the swell, we could look out the windows and see a wall of water at our level. Mind you, we were high up on the ferry, too.

To heck with that nonsense, we figured. We rented a small cabin that was simply equipped with double bunks and decided to sleep through the 100 mile crossing of the Cabot Strait.

It was the most terrible sea journey I'd ever experienced. We were all seasick to certain degrees, but one member of our party had an especially miserable voyage. He spent the entire seven hour trip in the latrine. Ironically, he was the most experienced sea traveler among us, having spent several years in the Navy.

We arrived at Port-au-Basques, Newfoundland just after dawn. The delicious feeling of solid ground meant more to us at that point than the upcoming adventure.

That tells you a lot about our state of mind from that awful ferry journey.

Wilfred Ryan greeted us cheerfully and asked how the trip had gone. Jim described the ferry ride and said he was not enthusiastic about the trip back home. Wilfred chuckled and reassured him that when he shot his big bull moose, the ferry ride would be easily forgotten. There was more truth than fiction to this statement, as we were to find out later.

As soon as we were introduced to Wilfred's wife, Carrie, and the three guides, Joachim, Thomas, and Eddy, we consumed a hearty breakfast and prepared immediately for the ride into camp. We learned that the hunting area was literally in Wilfred's back yard, although a rugged seven or eight mile ride on a pair of track vehicles was required to take us into camp.

While visiting in Wilfred's house, we noted that one of his young children who was about three years old was playing with a hunting knife. Of course, all of us were alarmed. Someone in our group called attention to it, but Wilfred's response was simple. "He knows about knives. Plays with them all the time."

We stowed our gear on a makeshift flat-bed trailer that would be towed by an all-terrain weasel. We would be riding in on another weasel, and Wilfred warned us that we were to hang on with both hands. After six miles of seemingly impassable terrain, we found out what he meant. At one point, a steep mountain loomed ahead and it appeared that it would easily defy the encroachment of any vehicle. I was certain that the gutted trail we were following would take advantage of contours and gradually climb the mountain, or at least gain elevation by a series of switchbacks, but I was wrong. The road punched straight up the mountain and topped out about a half mile above us.

In the last three hours of travel, I had misgivings about several parts of the road, especially the two rivers we'd crossed. Now, however, with the worst incline in front of us, I couldn't imagine climbing that steep slope, even though the presence of the road indicated it had been traversed before. Wilfred instructed us to ride as close to the front as possible to move the center of gravity forward. After several frightful minutes, the machines churned over the last of the grade and we had comparatively easy going the rest of the way.

The trip took about four hours and we reached camp by mid-afternoon. It was a comfortable looking sight and consisted of a main cookhouse-bunkhouse for hunters, a meatshed, and a storage building.

After settling into our bunkhouse, we joined Wilfred and the others at the dining table and discussed our plans.

Wilfred was optimistic. He told us he had guided 49 hunters that season, and 48 moose were taken. Though both bulls and cows are fair game, he told us that bulls made up the majority of the kill. He added that the only hunter that didn't score passed up a number of bulls in search of a trophy head.

Our only problem would be the weather, he contended. There were still hurricanes at large off the east coast and weather reports were not good. Wilfred said that if enough rain hit us we'd have to pull out early since the rivers we crossed would be raging torrents, and could keep us captive for days or even weeks.

After we were served hot tea, Wilfred explained how we would hunt. Jack, Fergie, and I would go out with Wilfred and Tom, while Jim and Bob would be guided by Eddy and Joachim. Each group would board a weasel well before sun-up each morning, and we would range out through the mountain for several miles. Then we'd leave the weasels and walk to selected areas to await the arrival of dawn.

The next morning showed little promise of a let-up in the weather. The wind howled all night and rain beat mercilessly without pause.

Carrie's tasty breakfast at 3:00 a.m. perked up our spirits, however, so we donned our raingear with high hopes. We climbed aboard the sides of the weasels and headed out for our hunting areas.

We hadn't gone one-quarter mile before my raingear was ripped thoroughly by sharp branches as we rolled through dense spruce thickets in the total darkness. The rain quickly permeated my clothing and I was soon soaked to the skin. We held on tightly to the roll bars and constantly ducked and swiveled to avoid the sharp, brittle needles of the spruce branches.

After an hour of seemingly endless travel, Wilfred brought the vehicle to a halt. We climbed down and followed him through the thick brush.

I'm all smiles with my first moose on my first moose hunt.

Dawn was approaching slowly and we began to make out the landscape in the improving light. I was impressed with the type of vegetation. A sea of almost impenetrable spruce stretched out in all directions. The trees were severely stunted and grew in uniform stands of the same height. Most of the trees were about chest high, although there were several stands that were 30 feet high or more. Small openings were interspersed in the vegetation, and occasional patches of alder dotted the gently rolling slopes.

Wilfred moved through the spruce thickets, or "tucks", as they are called locally, by following well used moose trails which meandered throughout the thick evergreen vegetation. He kept up a steady pace for about a half hour, and suddenly stopped before topping a rise. He cautioned us to move up slowly, and we carefully peered over the crest. Wilfred whispered that the valley below often produced moose. No animals were in sight, however, so we moved on again, stopping and glassing at each vantage point.

After three hours of this type of travel, the wind and rain picked up and hit us hard. The rain had changed from the steady, moderate tempo of the morning to a hammering downpour. Breathing was possible only by turning our backs to the wind. At times the gusts were so strong that we literally sank in the chest-high spruce for shelter.

Since I wear glasses, I was constantly wiping them to keep them dry, but to no avail. Finally, I took them off and gave up any hopes of spotting a moose. My scope needed constant wiping, too, because I don't use scope caps. I felt that the second or two it takes to yank them off may cost a shot at a fast disappearing target. It happened to me in the past. (Nowadays, modern caps can be removed quickly. I use them!)

We called it quits by noon, since we were spending more time huddling in the vegetation than hunting. We were so wet and miserable that we elected to forego lunch until we reached camp, even though we had to ride the weasel for a good hour.

When we arrived at the cabins, we learned that Jim and Bob were not back yet. Dry clothes and warm food helped our morale considerably, especially when Carrie's transistor radio forecasted more wind and rain for the next several days.

Everything seemed bleak and disappointing when we heard the other weasel pull into camp. I was in the bunkhouse cleaning my rifle when it arrived, and a series of shouts marked its approach. I looked out the door and saw a huge set of antlers tied to the roll bar, and jumped out into the mud barefooted. Jim Treacy beamed from ear to ear, so it was obvious who had scored.

After congratulations were passed around and we inspected the horns and carcass, we adjourned to the dining table and lis-

The late Jim Treacy with his big Newfoundland moose.

tened to Jim tell his story.

He and Bob had been following Eddy and Joachim for hours through the thickets, and they stopped periodically to glass areas from high points. At one rise, Eddy spotted something brown in the spruce. When the form of a moose rose under it, they realized they were looking at the top of an antler.

Apparently the moose either winded or heard them, because it spooked and broke for a small stand of tall timber that was nearby. Jim fired a round from his .30/06 as the moose passed between two trees. The bull faltered momentarily but recovered and gained the shelter of the timber. Jim sprinted for the other side of the trees and caught sight of the moose as it emerged from the stand, apparently headed for a much larger patch of timber. Jim fired again as the moose quartered away. The moose hit the ground at the shot but scrambled up and continued his flight. Jim touched off another round and knew the 180 grain handload had finished the job. The bull went down and didn't move.

Upon inspection of the carcass, they found that all three bullets had been good. The first two entered the chest cavity and the third hit squarely in the neck.

After dressing and quartering the moose, they carried it to a point where they could get at it with the weasel.

The time of the kill was about 10 a.m. Encouraged by this success, Bob Keegan wanted to continue hunting despite the wind and rain.

On two occasions, they flushed bulls, but each time only a snap shot was possible at the fleeing moose. Both times Bob was unable to fire in time.

When we awoke the next morning we discovered the rain had finally quit, but an extremely thick fog hung dense and heavy. Hopeful that the fog would lift, we boarded the weasels and started out again. Visibility was almost zero, and Wilfred had difficulty staying on the trail. The headlights on the weasel were useless.

For the first time, Wilfred expressed real concern. He was confident that the dense fog would remain for some time, so he suggested that we return to camp and wait for a break in the weather. We all agreed.

The weather did not break that day. The fog not only persist-
ed, but was periodically combined with heavy rains. We sat
around camp and made small talk, hoping for a bit of wind to
blow off the fog. Ironically enough, the day before we were
cussing the wind, but now we were praying for it.

At one point I couldn't stand the waiting any longer, so I
donned my raingear, uncased my .30/06, and decided to hunt
around camp. My efforts were in vain, however, because I
couldn't see 10 feet ahead of me. I backed up on my compass
bearing and returned to camp, groping through the fog-shroud-
ed timber.

More heavy rains commenced that evening and continued
through the night. The fog had lifted a bit but Wilfred had bad
news at the breakfast table. The radio had forecast another hurricane to be accompanied by more rain. It was due to hit in the
next 24 hours. Wilfred recommended that we break camp that
day, because the rivers we had to cross to get out would surely
be laden with flood waters.

It was heartbreaking news. Our anticipated six day hunt
would now be reduced to a total hunting time of one day, since
Wilfred wanted to be out by noon.

We had a half day to hunt, so we wasted no time in boarding
the weasels. The fog had thinned considerably, but wafted about
erratically.

We still-hunted for a few hours, but had no success. Wilfred
built a fire with some wood he carried along expressly for that
purpose, and boiled water. In a few minutes, we sipped hot tea
while huddling around the fire.

Wilfred had one more plan, and it was our last chance. He and
the other guides would make a drive through a big stand of timber after positioning us in good locations.

Wilfred directed me to a spot where three moose trails inter-
sected. When the party left and I stood there alone, I never felt
greater solitude in my life. It was the eeriest feeling I'd ever
experienced, and I'd spent time in the rain forests of the Pacific
Northwest and in wilderness areas of almost every western
state.

Perhaps the weirdest sensation was the absolute quiet.
Nothing stirred, there was no wind, and even the moisture-

laden evergreens were stark silent. The only movement was the fog, which wafted about like low-scudding clouds.

Suddenly, I had a startling sensation that something was watching me. I turned slowly to look behind me, but I saw nothing but a cloud of fog. As quietly as it had come, the fog drifted away, and I found myself staring face to face with a bull moose. The bull returned my stare fully, and it seemed that there was no other living thing in the world besides me and that moose.

After what seemed like hours, the staring match ended when the bull suddenly whirled and dashed for the timber. I shouldered the rifle, held just ahead of the bull's chest, and touched off a round.

A lone spruce tree shuddered when my bullet slammed into it. I thought the bullet would clear the tree when I fired, but I miscalculated when leading the running animal. There was no opportunity for another shot. The moose was in the timber unscathed.

Wilfred and the other guides emerged from the timber. I told them my story as we rounded up the other members of the party. Wilfred remarked that a staring contest with a bull moose was bad for any man's nerves.

We headed for camp and had given up all hopes. When we arrived, Carrie poured Jim and I a cup of hot tea. Since Jim had spent the morning in camp reading, I related the events of my experience. He offered his sympathy and suggested we head for the bunkhouse to pack our gear. When he started out the door, he spotted the moose drifting through camp.

The cabin immediately came alive. "Quick, Carrie," Wilfred whispered loudly, "Where's your rifle?"

Carrie ran into one of the back bedrooms while Wilfred and the guides ran into the other. The moose, meanwhile, meandered through the timber at a leisurely pace. He carried his head low and seemed to be carefully placing his feet down, as though he realized he had erred by approaching humans so closely, and was now trying to sneak away quietly.

I waited tensely and helplessly as the outfitter, his wife, and guides dashed about the rooms searching for the gun. I was sure the noise they were making would spook the moose, and I expected him to break any second. I fought the temptation to spring over to our bunkhouse, which was 40 feet away from the main cabin. My gun, as well as Jim's, was safely encased in the bunkhouse. Our other three companions were in the bunkhouse packing, completely unaware of what was happening.

I watched the moose nervously when someone shoved a rifle in my arms. Someone else jammed a single cartridge in my hand and prodded me out the door.

The moose was almost out of sight in the timber, so I pussy-footed around the back of the cabin, loading the rifle as I went. The shell didn't seat properly, so I feverishly worked the action until it closed smoothly. An immediate crashing sound from around the cabin indicated the moose heard my fumbling with the action and had spooked.

I ran around the corner of the cabin and heard him crashing through the timber, but I couldn't see him, so I sprinted for a high point where I hoped to catch a glimpse of him.

After a 200 yard run, which may have made the record books, I caught sight of the bull as he crossed a small clearing. I led him a bit and fired. The moose crumpled in his tracks and fell heavily to the ground.

I approached him cautiously but saw that no finishing shot was needed. The bullet took him through the chest and killed him instantly. I was delighted, of course, even though the moose had smallish antlers. At that point, any moose was a good moose.

A small crowd immediately formed around the moose and I. Jim, Wilfred, Carrie and the guides offered their congratulations.

A shout from the door of our bunkhouse caught our attention. Our three hunting companions were scrambling down to us to find out what was going on. Each of them showed looks of astonishment when they saw the moose.

They couldn't have been more astonished than I was. A few moments ago, I was sipping tea, ready to admit defeat, and preparing to pack for the long ride home. I couldn't believe that my luck changed from one extreme to the other. Just a few hours ago, I couldn't imagine anyone having worse luck, but with the help of Carrie's rifle, the moose that came to camp turned my adventure into one with a storybook ending.

But that's really not the end of the story. The ferry trip back was still ahead of us, and the winds were as fierce, if not worse, than the trip over. Then, too, there was the matter of crossing the now-swollen rivers between camp and Wilfred's house. Luckily, we made it out just in time. We barely got across, however, and there were times when we wondered if we'd be spending a week or two extra in the Newfoundland woods.

My old pickup is loaded with plenty of moose.

Before boarding the ferry I intended on buying some motion sickness pills, but we had met a hunter who wanted to ship a moose to some relatives in Nova Scotia, where we were headed. I volunteered to take the moose across in the bed of the truck, along with the other two, and forgot all about the pills. With the ship almost underway, I was most apprehensive about the crossing.

Luckily, I ran into a Canadian sailor just before the ferry was to leave the dock, and he had one Dramamine pill left. He generously offered it to me, and I warmly accepted.

I took the pill and immediately laid down and went to sleep in a cabin. Waking up eight hours later, I assumed we'd crossed the Cabot Strait and had sailed into the harbor at Nova Scotia. Wrong. We had not even left Newfoundland, because the ocean was too rough. The miserable journey was still ahead of us, and I'd already taken the pill which after eight hours had used up its value.

You can believe I said to heck with that boat ride. Next time, I'm flying.

NOTE -- Some years later, a ferry capsized in rough seas on the route we'd taken. I believe it was the same ferry we'd ridden on. Regrettably, there was a very high loss of life.

I'LL HAVE MY SHEEP RIBS
MEDIUM RARE

The trail is etched into the Wyoming mountainside, winding up toward the ridgetop miles away. Our horses climb easily, cautiously making their way along the narrow path. With luck, we'll be at base camp around dark.

Camp is in one of the most remote wilderness areas in the lower 48 states. According to outfitter Nate Vance, it nestles in a valley 35 miles from the trailhead. We've been in the saddle for several hours, and have another seven to eight hours of riding to look forward to. In order to help exercise my muscles and give the horse a break, I dismount occasionally and lead the horse downhill whenever possible.

The trail has the look of hard use. Countless horse's hooves have bitten into the soil, creating a narrow avenue that accesses the remote country. You know the journey is basically safe, but every now and then you see where hooves tore off part of the downhill edge of the trail, and you wonder if it was a pack animal or a saddle horse that almost plummeted into oblivion below. Then too, you are unfortunately aware of mishaps along this trail where animals have indeed gone off the edge. In some cases, humans had close calls on those lofty pathways, and you hope you and your horse have a completely uneventful and boring trip.

The perils of the ride are easily offset by the magnificence of the country you pass through. Limber pine trees seem impossibly anchored to slopes so steep that you know there can't be any worthwhile soil around the roots. Rocks and boulders decorated with red, orange, yellow, and lime-green lichens seem to have been painted by a wild artist wielding a frenzied brush.

But the air makes it so special — sweet, crisp mountain air that appears to be innocent of the foul and filthy skies that smother much of the rest of the world. Here it is pure, though containing less oxygen than you'd find in most civilized elevations. Because of that oxygen deficit, you feel a bit lightheaded in the 10,000-foot air, but it's an okay feeling. It's worth it.

As you ride, you muse about the objective of all this travel in the high country. Somewhere ahead, miles ahead, you picture a bighorn sheep that you hope will soon become part of your life. You hope for the biggest ram in Wyoming, of course, but that's not necessary. A legal ram must have three-quarter curl – a ram of that stature will do just fine.

Finally the long-awaited ridge is just ahead. The horses seem to know it's coming, as they climb upward with a bit more energy and enthusiasm. We are about to approach the much cussed – and discussed, Deer Creek Pass.

Nate points out a trio of snow shovels leaning against a rock. They are useless now on the bare ground, and Nate brings you up to date on their past performance.

"This trail is open only a couple months out of the year," Nate volunteers when he sees you staring at the shovels. "Most of the time we need to shovel out four to six feet of snow to punch through."

You think about that statement, and picture Nate and his guides working feverishly to clear a path over the ridge. You smile when you consider Nate's lifestyle. How many humans consider it part of a day's work to shovel snow at 10,000 feet in a remote region where physical strength and endurance are prerequisites to survival?

A group of Rocky Mountain bighorns in typical high elevation habitat.

Deer Creek Pass is a major obstacle in much of the region's wilderness country. At times the snow is several feet deep on the Fourth of July. Your access into this enormous backcountry is entirely dependent on the pass. If you can get through, you're in good shape. If not, you must find another entry – some outfitters drive more than 100 miles to other trailheads.

Darkness is descending rapidly as we enter a long valley. This is the famous Thoroughfare region, a legendary big game utopia visited by hunters for more than 100 years. Mention the Thoroughfare to an avid sheep or elk hunter, and you'll be talking a household term.

As we ride toward the Thoroughfare, I can't help but think about Jack O'Connor, the legendary writer who was OUTDOOR LIFE's Shooting and Hunting editor some years before I went to work for OUTDOOR LIFE. Jack had visited the region a number of times, hunting sheep and elk, and I read his stories with rapt attention. What I remember most is his reference to sheep ribs cooked over a campfire. How I want to duplicate that feast!

Nate and I are accompanied on our long horseback trip by several of his hands who are heading in to base camp which serves as elk hunting headquarters, as well as two video producers. Bill Grunkmeyer and an assistant are with us to photograph my hunt. This will be most interesting – coping with several hundred pounds of camera gear and all the inherent problems that go with photography at the high 10,000 foot elevation where we'll be hunting.

Pine-scented woodsmoke tips us off to the presence of Nate's camp long before we arrive. Somewhere in the darkness a group of tents will provide shelter from the wilderness. The plan is to eat dinner, relax, and get a good night's sleep before riding out to spike camp in the morning.

Sleep. Who can sleep amidst the excitement and expectations of the days ahead? Though I'm bone-tired from riding and walking for 35 miles, I'm not so sure sleep will come easy.

Finally our horses step into an opening where we see a sliver of lantern light through the trees. The light seems suddenly foreign, as out of place here as a Cadillac. The brightness somehow steals the exquisite peace in the darkness that seemed to grow more friendly as the evening wore on.

The idea of civilization, no matter how tiny in that backcountry valley, is finally welcome as I realize I've had all the horse riding a person can want in a day. Warm dinner would be nice, and maybe the sleeping bag will be enticing after all.

Light from many lanterns show Nate's camp to be tidy, tucked away unobtrusively into the forest. We unload the packhorses and place our personal belongings in the sleeping tent. I note that the cot looks comfortable, and remind myself that this is but a one-night stop. Tomorrow we'll ride another eight or nine miles higher yet into the mountains. The spike camp that we'll erect there will have none of the amenities of the base camp. A small tent and a campfire will shelter us and provide the bare essentials required to survive.

"See any grizzlies on the way in?" the cook asks after greetings are passed around.

"Not a thing," Nate responds. "Any action around here?"

"Saw that dark-colored boar this morning," the cook says. "Up on the bench behind the horse corral."

Nate mutters something about bears and I marvel about the nonchalant attitude toward grizzlies. Like it happens almost every day. Which it does. Grizzlies and the Wyoming backcountry are as old as time. Nate seems to be indifferent about their presence, but I know he's acutely aware of them. Living with grizzlies requires alertness. You must pay attention.

After putting away a fabulous dinner, I'm shown to a special tent. The inside walls are almost completely filled with writings and art left by former occupants. Some verses are a few lines long, amounting to a thank you for a hunt. Others are longer sonnets, in poetry and prose formats. All are reminders of the past, of other humans who rode the same trail as I, saw the same rocks, trees, and bejeweled mountaintops. Nate points to a blank spot on the tent wall that is reserved for my comments at hunt's end. As I head for my cot in my sleeping tent, I wonder what I could write about. It's a thought worth pondering, but finally my brain gives up. Morning will come too soon.

The trail in to spike camp is primitive, requiring us to walk our horses over, around, and under serious obstacles. Making matters worse, ominous clouds in the west threaten severe weather. Since it is late August, we aren't terribly concerned about snow, which is nonetheless a possibility. The concern is lightning, intense bolts that hammer the high country on almost a daily basis this time of year. Our little camp will be set on a ridgetop, an open invitation for a lightning strike. And, of course, we worry about Bill's elaborate camera gear. We don't want it to get wet, and because there's no electricity in the wilderness (generators are forbidden), the batteries must be continually charged by solar power.

The tents go up rapidly, but the storm hits before we're done. Rain, hail, and powerful wind gusts hamper our efforts, hastening our attempts to get camp up and going. Finally, a cheery campfire dries our clothes as we watch the flashing electrical theatre drift off into the east.

My first sheep, taken high in the most remote area of the lower 48.

Meals are not to be gourmet delights, and for good reason. We are programmed into thinking grizzlies every step of the way, which essentially means keeping food odors minimized. We eat canned food, and take no chances, hanging it 15 feet high from the limb of a tree.

As we stare at the campfire's flames that night, Nate and I are

A ram jumps off a ledge, making it look like child's play.

deep into our personal thoughts. I envision big rams standing regally on every precipice, and imagine all of us feasting on sheep ribs some night soon. Nate nudges me back into reality by suggesting we reinforce the campfire with a huge pitchy stump that will burn brightly all night. I ask the dumb question why, and Nate's response is about what I expected.

"The Yellowstone Park border is only a mile away," Nate says. "That's the deepest, most remote part of the park, and that happens to be the spot where they dump the bad grizzlies. The bold ones that get into trouble with people."

Great. That kind of news isn't exactly what I want to hear, but it's best to be prepared. Nate will get no quarrel from me. Indeed we'll drag a big pitchy stump into the fire, and I know exactly where my rifle will be tonight.

No grizzly bear attacks us as we sleep, and we awaken long before the earliest splashes of morning light. Our horses are saddled after we have a quick breakfast, but we delay our departure until the skies brighten. I'm edgy, wanting to go, not sure where, but to be heading for a ram somewhere in that godawful high and lonely country. After all, it's opening morning.

Nate senses my eagerness, and offers an explanation to our waiting game with the sun.

"Our camp is smack in the middle of sheep country," he says. "I've had hunters kill rams within 300 yards of our tent. Let's not be too hasty to ride out."

No problem, old buddy. If wait we must, then so be it. I figure I've already paid my dues by surviving the riding and hiking into spike camp. A ram taken at fireside will not lessen the enormity of the hunt, but I have a hunch that we're in for some profound exercise.

What happens next is so impossible that my mind initially refuses to comprehend the sight before my eyes. A ram exits the trees bordering camp and strolls about with not a care in the world. It isn't a legal ram, but others may follow.

I waste no time grabbing my rifle and settling in on a solid rest. Damn. Sheep season is open, and here is a sheep next to camp. Maybe this hunt will end here after all.

It is not to be. No other ram shows up, which is no major disappointment. Suddenly it seems that to kill my ram next to camp will be cheating myself out of the whole experience. I'm ready to get back in, deeper yet into the wild heights.

Our horses can go no farther. Scree slopes fall away into deep canyons, trails are hospitable only to game. We tie our animals to stunted pines and slip up to the edge of a rim. In no time we see sheep, including a good ram. He is below us, out of rifle range, but approachable. For a long time we scrutinize his horns and decide to pass. We reason that it's only opening morning; bigger rams should be available.

Now we begin to hunt, to REALLY hunt. Carrying light-weight daypacks, we hike up steep slopes, slide down the other side, glass, hike, and slide some more. I swear there is not a flat spot in that part of Wyoming, and most of our travel is in uphill fashion. The air that seemed to be so sweet and pure when we rode in to base camp is now thin and sickening. I gasp in lung-fuls, fully expecting my lungs to burst. I rationalize that this is no surprise, is completely what I expected, but on the other hand, is an extraordinary experience. I'm no stranger to strenu-ous mountain hunting, and in fact live barely 40 miles away as the crow flies, but this is a novel adventure. Having a sheep tag in my pocket makes it totally unique. But it is physical. Totally.

The photo crew is having a tough time as well, lugging a large assemblage of camera gear, film, and batteries. They're with us every step of the way to document the hunt on film.

Our horses are welcome sights as we trudge back after our hard session in the rocks. No other sheep are spotted that day, and I'm an early candidate for the sleeping bag. Sleep comes instantly tonight.

More rough days follow, each seemingly tougher than the previous. Logically the hunting should get easier as the body toughens, but Nate is relentless in the search for our ram. He continues to push farther and farther, deeper and deeper from our tied horses. We see sheep every day, but no legal rams.

The grizzlies compound our problems. We haven't seen a bear yet, but their fresh signs betray their presence in and around camp, day and night. We continue to follow routine precautions, including the ritual of searching for, digging out, and dragging a pitchy stump to our campfire each night.

The weather continues to be fickle and unpredictable, as it

Nate Vance packs out my ram (covered with protective cloth). This is unforgiving country.

does in the high country, and turns cooler. Snow falls intermittently, but not enough to coat the ground and help us spot sheep.

One day I make a great find. My eyes spot something out of place on the ground. I pick it up, and to my surprise, it's an Indian arrowhead. I can't believe my good luck. For years I've searched for arrowheads, and even though my companions would spot them, my only success was to locate chips and pieces. I'd long ago said to heck with arrowhead hunting, but here was a perfect artifact. Perhaps it was a good omen.

Glassing is our primary strategy. We sit for an hour or more, looking through a spotting scope. Sometimes I experience a roaring headache from so much intense focusing through the optics, but luckily the headaches diminish quickly. That's a complication I don't need.

Finally, on a brisk morning that promises to be lovely, Nate spots three sheep far below us. I'm gazing off into another canyon, watching the fog rising in huge masses when he makes the discovery.

One of the rams is acceptable, not a candidate for the record book, or even close, but plenty good for me. We watch for a long time, until one of the sheep beds down on a slope. The other two follow, all of them within sight.

It's time to make the move. The big move. All the months of preparation and anticipation are about to be terminated. That is, if we do our job well.

Carefully checking the wind, Nate and I drop out of sight. The camera crew follows, as always. Our goal is a ledge about 200 yards from the sheep. If we can reach it without being observed by our quarry, this hunt should be history.

Our worst fears come true. A rock tumbles from underfoot, alerting the bedded sheep. They're up on their feet instantly, dashing around the ledge. Nate suddenly sprints forward, and I do likewise. With any luck, we can cut the sheep off and be in a position above them for a shot.

My lungs are on fire, but we run, jumping and clambering over rocks. Bill is right behind me, somehow carrying the big camera and maintaining his balance. Suddenly Nate halts, pointing to the trio of running sheep. They're 175 yards out, going straight away.

I quickly chamber a round, lay the .30/06 on a rock, draw a bead on the ram, and touch the trigger. The rifle explodes, and the sheep lurches, hit hard. Somehow he stays on his feet, and I hit him again, this time putting him down for good.

It takes us 20 minutes to work our way around to the ram. Upon approaching him I'm mesmerized by his presence. The very idea of taking the ram overwhelms me. The size of his respectable horns are secondary to the fact that I'd finally achieved a lifetime fantasy of experiencing a superb mountain adventure.

On another happy note, Bill is all smiles. He tells us he got everything on film, an amazing feat, what with all the running and commotion on the steep, rocky mountain slope.

Yes, the sheep ribs were sensational, just as I'd expected. Combined with tenderloins that we'd cooked in bacon grease, potatoes, and beans, it was indeed a meal fit for a king.

The finale of the hunt, however, wasn't quite over when Nate and I and the camera crew packed up and headed down to base camp. There was the matter of the tent with the empty spot on the wall. It was my turn to inscribe my feelings. That was easy to do.

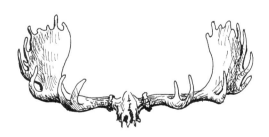

DID I REALLY SHOOT A COW?

If you think buffalo are stupid animals with half a brain, as I once did, then you haven't been around the wild herd of buffalo in Utah's Henry Mountains. Those animals are truly wild, unconfined by fences, and hunted regularly. Being a Utah resident for years, I'd heard about these animals frequently, but I'd never seen them first hand.

As good luck would have it, that all changed when I drew a bison tag in 1981. I was pretty happy with myself because a couple years before I'd also drawn a Utah desert bighorn sheep tag. Each of these are once in a lifetime animals, that is, once you draw a tag you're done, whether you get an animal or not. The hunt success rate for buffalo (also known as bison) runs about 95 percent as I recall, and not necessarily because the animals are easy to hunt, but because it's a fairly long season. If you work hard enough you can usually find one.

Of course, my sights were set on a bull bison, but either sex was allowed because both have horns and they look enough alike that it can be difficult to tell them apart. Mistaking a cow for a bull is common.

It so happened that a writer friend of mine from the east coast had planned to hunt with me that same fall. Rick Methot had won some cash in a writer's contest, allowing him to buy a plane ticket and hunt with me. These plans were all made long before I learned that I'd drawn a buffalo tag. When I told Rick about the buffalo, he was as happy for me as I was, and had no problem with tagging along for the first few days of the buffalo season.

The plan was to hunt buffalo for a few days, and then to go to South Dakota to the Governor's Pheasant Hunt which included a number of writers, and then to come back to Colorado where I'd guide Rick on a mule deer hunt. All in all, Rick would be in the West for about two weeks. I figured that if I didn't get my buffalo on the first three days of the season with Rick, then we'd do our other hunts and I'd finish up later after Rick left.

Rick flew into Vernal, Utah where I lived, and together we went down to the Henry Mountains which are in the southern part of the state. These are rugged mountains. The buffalo live in the basins, the desert, mountain slopes, and in the pinion juniper forests where they've got plenty of escape cover. Of course, having been born and raised there, these huge animals indeed know how to escape.

Prior to the hunt, it was mandatory to attend an orientation meeting where wildlife officers instructed you on how to help them test the buffalo for brucellosis. What we had to do was obtain blood from the animal as well as some stomach contents because the biologists wanted data on what the buffalo were eating. They gave us a couple of vials to put blood in, and a plastic bag to hold some of the stomach contents. They also told us where we might find some buffalo, where to aim for a killing shot, and some other interesting details. Among them were ways to tell a bull from a cow buffalo. Both animals, the biologists claimed, have humps on their backs, but the bulls tended to have bigger humps, although that could be hard to tell in the field. They said a sure fire way is to look for the penile sheath which definitely indicates the bull from the cow.

I look for buffalo in typical Utah habitat.

Rick and I parked the camper in a likely spot and headed out early on opening morning. We hiked around for a good share of the morning but didn't see any buffalo. We did, however, run into a few other hunters.

At one point, we talked to a hunter who said that he'd met another hunter who had shot a big bull buffalo. Another big bull stood next to the fallen animal, refusing to leave it. The hunter that was talking to us had taken his animal already and told us where we might find the other hunter and the two bulls. Evidently this party had discovered a small herd of buffalo.

We walked off in the direction that he told us to follow, and we worked our way out on a rocky overlook that was grown over with fairly thick pinion trees.

I spotted a hunter kneeling down with a rifle at the ready, looking intently at a prone buffalo that was lying about two feet away from a cliff. Another big bull, very much alive, was standing motionless next to the fallen animal. Both buffalo were no more than 30 yards away.

I eased up to the hunter, a woman who was with her husband. She whispered that she didn't want to startle the buffalo that she'd hit because she wasn't sure if it was dead. If it jumped up it would surely go over the cliff and fall about 200 feet. The lady would have a whole lot of buffalo burger on her hands. Wisely, she opted to wait and to see what would happen.

In the meantime, she explained that another hunter had been waiting with her and her husband, but had made a little circle to see if he could find yet another bull. Evidently the other hunter was also nervous about the cliff, worried that his also might plummet over the edge.

It goes without saying that I was most interested in the bull, but it seemed that since the other hunter had gotten there first, it was best to wait. Some courtesy was required, even though I was probably within the bounds of good ethics to shoot, once the woman had given the go-ahead. The other hunter had told the woman and her husband that he'd be right back.

Fifteen minutes later we all determined that the bull lying on the ground was dead. We looked at it with binoculars, and could see no movement at all. The other buffalo still stood alongside the dead bull.

The other hunter came back and decided to take the big bull where it stood. He did. Hit hard, the animal ran about 10 yards, luckily away from the cliff, and dropped. Now the party of hunters had their work cut out for them. They had friends standing by at camp to help them pack their meat out. I hope they had big, husky pals, possibly all-star tackles from the NFL. There was a bunch of meat to be moved that day.

Rick and I hunted the rest of that day, and for the next two days, and never saw another buffalo. We had only talked to about six hunters who had scored (I believe there were about 25 tags issued for the area).

Rick and I left the Henry Mountains, headed for the other hunts. We drove to South Dakota, had a great time, got all the pheasants the law allowed, and met some wonderful people. From there we drove back to Colorado where we hunted for mule deer. Rick saw a monster buck, but it was running into the sun and he couldn't get a shot at it. The glare blocked vision through his scope; unfortunately, that spelled the end of his hunt.

With Rick gone, I needed to find someone else to hunt with me. It's not very prudent to hunt buffalo alone for obvious reasons (I'm not an all-star tackle). I called my old pal Doug McKnight who owned a sporting goods store in St. George, Utah. Elsewhere in this book you'll read a chapter about a pick-up truck that burned up in the desert on a sheep hunt. That was Doug's truck, and the incident had happened a couple of years before this buffalo hunt.

Doug agreed to hunt buffalo with me. He was that kind of guy, always ready to go at a moment's notice. He loved to hunt as much as I did and he was great company to have along.

We were a bit concerned about the hunt because from all the reports we'd gotten, the animals were tucked into the pinion-juniper forest and were hard to find. There were still about a dozen people who hadn't gotten their buffalo yet, and only a couple of days were left in the season. I had been wrong big time when I thought that two or three days would be enough. Evidently they were not.

It's not a bull, but I'm pleased with my buffalo.

On the first day we hunted, Doug and I drove out into an area called a chaining. This is a vegetative treatment, commonly known as a habitat improvement project. A huge ship anchor chain is dragged between two bulldozers. All the pinyon and juniper trees are uprooted and windrowed or burned. The cleared area is then planted with a variety of seeds which produce nutritious forage, benefiting wildlife and livestock.

Doug and I had worked our way into the middle of a dense pinion juniper forest that was adjoined by a clearing. We saw some dust coming up from a small opening and moved up closer to investigate.

Doug McKnight skins my buffalo. It took several hours to process the carcass.

It was a sight to behold. About 45 buffalo were wallowing about; they were at least 600 yards away. The wind was shifting here and there but we didn't think much of it because the animals were so far off. Frankly, we didn't really think that they'd be that wary of our scent.

Wrong. Somehow those animals detected our presence and started to run. I'm talking here about a good, old-fashioned, buffalo stampede, the kind you see on TV and read about in the Wild West days. These animals were running full-out. They were not fooling around.

The herd raced through the trees, and Doug and I broke out of the pines and got up onto some stumps in the chaining. It appeared that the buffalo were confused and were going to run at an angle where we might get a glimpse at them.

When we realized what direction they were headed in, Doug and I took off again, trying to head them off at the pass. It was easy to keep track of the herd; they'd give a freight train competition in the noise department.

A final sprint put Doug and I in a position that might work, though I was breathing so hard from running that I'd need to concentrate hard if a shot presented itself.

It did. Moments later the stampeding herd of buffalo turned toward us. I can tell you right now that watching and hearing those animals, and feeling the ground literally shake beneath my feet was the thrill of a lifetime. As the buffalo ran past us in a big bunch, I frantically looked for the boss bull of the herd. Doug and I traded information back and forth as we looked over all the animals, and finally I saw one large buffalo that looked like it had a big hump. I couldn't see any penile sheath since there wasn't any time and there was too much dust. The animal was off just a bit by itself along the perimeter of the herd when I took one shot with my .30/06. I heard the bullet hit but I had no clue how much damage it had done.

"Shoot it again," Doug said.

Suddenly that particular buffalo was caught up in the midst of others and I couldn't tell which one I had shot at. There was no way I could shoot again because I certainly didn't want to hit two animals. The herd had traveled another 50 yards, when all of a sudden a single animal just sort of peeled off from the group, did a little spiral, and fell over to the ground. My buffalo hunt was over.

Doug loped over to the animal first and I was trailing right behind. He lifted up one leg of the animal and said, "Zumbo, it's got udders."

I'd shot a cow, a great big old cow buffalo. I can't say I was really disappointed, given the fact that I hadn't planned this hunt very well and had grossly underestimated the time I'd need to locate a big bull. But I'd finally gotten my buffalo, and I was happy with it.

Now the chore was to get it out. My truck was parked about a half a mile away, and I thought I might be able to weave in and around the chaining to get fairly close to the carcass. I should mention that my pickup was brand new and had only about 3,000 miles on it. I started in, picking my way carefully, driving around the windrowed piles of branches and trees. I was about 150 yards away from the buffalo when I heard a loud thunk. One of my tires had hit a stout branch just right. The branch flipped up and whacked the quarter panel of my truck, leaving a deep gouge. So much for my pretty truck, and for my savings account (Doug was glad he wasn't driving). I figured it would cost about $500 to fix it, which was the amount of my deductible, and I muttered something about bad luck for trucks when Doug and I hunt together.

Doug and I spent the next six hours sawing and skinning the buffalo. I wanted to try to take it out in quarters if possible. We finally got the job done, loaded up the quarters, and drove over to my camper. Soon we had the meat hanging in a tree to cool, and I'll admit that Doug's bumper winch was mighty helpful in hoisting the quarters over a stout branch.

The next morning I gave half the buffalo to Doug and headed home. The buffalo meat was just as I'd expected, – fantastic. If I ever have a chance to get another I can assure you I will. I'll never say to heck with buffalo hunting, but next time I'll try a little harder to see that doggone penile sheath.

NOW I KNOW HOW
A POPSICLE FEELS

The Shiras moose is one of the three moose species in North America and also happens to be the smallest of the three. But, come on! Can you really consider a 1,000 pound moose to be small?

Anyway, this subspecies lives in the Rocky Mountains; most of them in Wyoming. In fact, the Shiras is often called the Wyoming moose. Other states with good populations include Montana, Idaho, Utah and now Colorado after a recent transplant in the late 1970's.

Living in Wyoming, as I do, doesn't necessarily mean that it's easy to draw a moose tag, despite the fact that about 1,000 tags

147

are offered each year. In every state, tags are offered in a lottery draw. The odds of drawing vary with the particular unit you're applying for, depending on the popularity of that unit. Units are popular if they have good access and big moose. You can bet that your chances of drawing in those areas will be much tougher than those that don't offer larger bulls.

I was hoping to increase my odds as much as possible, and it didn't matter what kind of moose was available; the objective was moose meat. I should explain here that being an outdoor writer specializing in big game hunting, there's a bit of pressure to trophy hunt, especially if I'm with an outfitter. But when I'm on my own, the pressure is off. That's when I really enjoy the hunt in all its aspects -- antlers aren't important.

I called my good pal, Dr. Harry Harju, who was the chief biologist for the Wyoming Game and Fish Department, and asked if he had any suggestions for decent odds on drawing a moose tag, any moose. Harry suggested an area that had mostly private land and few good bulls. About 85 percent of this unit is in private ownership and most of the bulls taken are small animals with 20 to 25 inch racks. Cows are also allowed with an either-sex tag.

I applied for the tag along with my son-in-law, Matt Inkster. Matt lived in Laramie with my daughter Judi; they were both attending the University of Wyoming. As great luck would have it, Matt and I each drew either-sex moose tags. We were both amazed, and of course, excited. It appeared that moose meat was about to become a reality in our freezers.

We didn't know where to start hunting, since both of us were unfamiliar with the unit, so we took a drive out to the area in the summer to have a general look at the landscape. We learned that most of the ranchers in the area were happy to allow moose hunters. The big animals weren't very well liked because they raided crops and destroyed haystacks. For that reason, many landowners wanted to get rid of as many moose as possible.

Our trip helped us determine terrain, vegetation, and access. My youngest daughter, Angie, went along, as did Matt and Judi. We did a little fishing and had a long, relaxing weekend. Moose sign seemed plentiful, and we had high hopes.

As it turned out, Matt had some college commitments for

opening day of the moose season, and I also had a conflict. We couldn't make the opening week of the hunt, but I wasn't concerned, since plenty of moose seemed to be available.

Matt and Dan glass for moose in the willow bottom.

We started on our trip about 10 days after the season opened. My son, Dan, went along with us. I brought my Jayco camp trailer but still didn't have any specific idea where we were going. I planned on meeting Matt and Dan at a town near the unit. On the way to the moose hunt, I stopped at a gas station and talked with a hunter who had just shot a moose in our unit.

He told me about a particular rancher who had lots of moose and was very anxious to have as many removed as possible. I immediately went to a phone, called the ranch, and talked to the foreman. No problem getting permission to hunt. "Shoot all the moose you see." he said. When he detected a slight pause in my voice, he added: "Just kidding, but I'd sure like to see a lot less moose on the ranch." The foreman told us we could park my camper near the ranch house.

Matt, Danny and I got camp set up just at dark on the day before we were to start hunting. We didn't have a chance to look the area over, but the ranch foreman told us there were moose all over the place, even though a half dozen had been killed by hunters since the season had opened.

Matt had only two days to hunt, and that would probably be it for the entire season. He's a musician and had a number of commitments and conflicts, so it wasn't easy to get time off. As I already mentioned, this was a meat hunt for both of us, so it didn't really matter that we didn't see a big bull moose. Any old moose would be just fine.

We got up early the next morning and wandered through a big willow swamp next to pasturelands that held cattle. In the next two hours, we saw at least seven cow and calf moose but no bulls. We had decided to look for bulls the first day and if nothing happened, Matt would take a cow the second day. I still had plenty of time to hunt, intending on returning later if I had to. The tail end of the season would undoubtedly be much colder with a lot more snow on the ground, offering better moose hunting conditions.

We didn't see a bull on that first day, but on the second morning after hunting for about two hours and seeing several cows, I spotted a spike bull. As they say, any moose is a good moose, especially if it's standing close to the road. This bull wasn't really close to the road although he was maybe 300 yards away, but I had my handy one-wheeled game carrier, a Pac'Orse, that would do the job nicely.

Matt decided to take the bull and dropped him nicely with one shot. With the three of us working steadily, we had the animal completely field-dressed, skinned and quartered in about three hours. After packing the meat in large meat bags and cutting the horns off, we had everything loaded in my truck by 1:00 in the afternoon. Matt was happy, I was happy, and Dan was happy. One moose down; one to go.

Matt's moose is no giant, but it was fabulous on the dinner table.

I decided to leave because Dan had to go back to his job, and Matt had to return to Laramie. I had an elk hunt that week, but I was looking forward to moose hunting when there was deeper snow and I could do some tracking. I had an idea there might be some bigger bulls in the area.

I returned to the ranch a couple of weeks later, again pulling my camper and parking it in the same spot. I hunted hard in the snow but only saw a half dozen cows and calves. I had some fun calling and was able to attract a number of moose, but no bulls. I had decided to take the first decent bull that came along, although I had three more days to hunt.

I also had purchased three doe mule deer tags. The state was offering many tags in the area because there was an overabundance of deer and I wanted to use the meat to make some sausage and jerky.

Matt (left) and Dan wheel out the moose meat, using a Pac'Orse.

I took two deer on the second morning. It was very cold out, about 15 degrees below zero, so as soon as I had the deer dressed and in my truck they were frozen as hard as rocks a couple hours later.

The moose hunting was still the same as usual. Cows were consistently seen, but no bulls. It was about 3:00 in the afternoon the day before the last day when I ran into the rancher. I hadn't met him before; I'd just talked to his wife and the foreman. The rancher was a man known for few words, but when he said something you'd better pay attention. He was also known to be a bit on the gruff side.

When he pulled up alongside me next to the road, he lowered his window and said, "I just saw a big head."

I said, "What do you mean?"

"I just saw a big head, biggest moose I've ever seen in twenty-five years," he responded.

I felt a little foolish to ask him how big the moose was because if it was a big head to this man who lived around moose all his life, it would certainly be a big head to me. My momma didn't raise no fool. I thanked him for the tip, and asked where he'd seen it. He allowed as to how he'd spotted it near one of the pastures when he was rounding up cows that morning.

With only a couple hours that day and one more day to go, there was no choice. I went to look for the bull although he was last seen near a nasty willow bottom full of beaver dams. I hunted until dark and saw a cow and a calf, nothing else.

The next morning I went back into the swamp and still saw nothing. I had an idea this bull was probably moving since he hadn't been seen in that area before. I did a lot of hiking, crisscrossing back and forth, looking for tracks bigger than others, and penetrating the densest willow hide-outs I could find. I turned up no bull, or sign of him, and something told me that the moose had just been passing through. I had about an hour left of daylight and moose season would be over. I was plenty concerned that I might not get any moose, not even a cow. I hadn't seen one at all that day.

There was about 20 minutes of light left when suddenly I saw a big cow. I looked at her through binoculars, noted that she did not have a calf, and then had to make a decision. I was a long way from the truck at this point, and it was very cold, about 20 degrees below zero. I knew that if I dropped this moose I'd be out there working for a long time in the dark and that there'd be no way to get her out that night.

But I really had no choice. It was either this old girl or nothing. I aimed behind her shoulder, fired, and she dropped at the spot.

In my haste to get to her, instead of running in the brush and on solid land, I tried to take a short-cut across a small beaver pond that I thought was covered with thick ice. After all, it had been well below zero for several days. My mistake. I hit some thin ice and plunged through. My left leg went down all the way to the top of my thigh. The water was only a couple of feet deep so I was able to spring back out, but nonetheless that leg was soaked and I knew I might be in trouble if I didn't hurry. I immediately thought of a buddy of mine, 25 years ago when I was in forestry school, who had gotten in a similar situation. He'd gone through a beaver dam with both legs (it was 20 below zero), and by the time he got out of the woods several hours later we had to rush him to the hospital. He almost lost both legs. As luck would have it, he only suffered frostbite in a couple of his toes. Now it was also about 20 degrees below zero. But my friend had been out for a long time, trying to drag a big whitetail buck in deep snow. I reasoned that it would only take me a half hour to dress this moose and probably another half hour to get back to the truck. Not to worry, I told myself.

I didn't want to waste any time when I reached the cow, dressing her as quickly as I could. I'll admit it was a sloppy job, but I got everything out that had to come out in about 15 minutes. You've never seen such a knife exhibition as I cut and tore with reckless abandon. I propped her belly open and had to finish the job with a flashlight. Luckily there were stars and moon to help guide my way, because my flashlight was getting dimmer. I always carry two flashlights, but on that particular hunt I didn't because I had used one on the previous hunt and didn't replace the batteries. Dumb move. Because the stars and moon were out, it was much colder than if it was cloudy, but at least they provided some light.

I headed back for the truck and could feel my left leg starting to become numb. My jeans were frozen solid; it was all I could do to bend my leg at the knee to walk. I hurried along as fast as I could, realizing that I could be in big time serious trouble. I trotted as much as possible to the truck, but in the willow swamp I had to jump from hummock to hummock and I was doing this with the aid of a weak flashlight and with the moon and starlight. My stiff left leg was practically useless. I did a lot more stumbling sideways than moving forward. Finally I got to where I thought the truck should be by looking at landmarks. Then I saw the moonlight gleam off the glass of the truck about 200 yards ahead and I hurried even faster. By then my left leg was really starting to hurt and my jeans were so frozen that I had to keep that left leg almost stiff as I made my way. I ran as fast as I could, hopping on the one foot that I could bend with the aid of a stick that I'd found.

When I got to the truck I was so cold and my teeth were chattering so badly I knew I was in the early stages of hypothermia. My hands seemed to be almost frozen solid – when I had been working in the moose's cavity the warm blood had frozen to my hands afterward. I tried to wash some of the blood off with snow but that only made it worse. When I put my gloves on my hands never really warmed up.

Now I was at the truck fumbling for the keys. Try as I might, I couldn't turn the key in the ignition; my hands were so paralyzed with cold. Finally, with all the strength I could muster, I gritted my teeth, and by using both hands, I managed to start the engine. All the while I had to push down with my frozen left leg as hard as I could to press the clutch pedal to the floor. For sure I said to heck with manual shift right then and there.

I just sat huddled there in the cab and waited for the truck to warm up. Finally, after what seemed like an eternity, I felt heat, wonderful, fabulous heat. My hands slowly started to thaw and I felt like I could drive, but my left leg was still pretty much encased in ice.

I drove back to town, realizing that I needed to get into a hot bathtub. Instead of going to the camper that had little or no heat, I checked into a motel and quickly and carefully removed my frozen clothes. What followed was one of the most wonderful hot baths of my life. Luckily, I suffered no permanent problems, though I didn't sleep well that night due to a tingling sensation in my left leg and my fingers.

The next morning I went back out to my camper and got some fresh clothes, all the gear I needed, and headed back out to the moose. I took my skinning knives, boning knives, meat saw, meat sacks, and of course, my one wheeled carrier.

I couldn't get the carrier quite to the moose because of the obstacles in the swamp, but I did manage to get it about 400 yards away. Once at the moose, I carefully skinned her, having a hard job of it because most of the carcass was frozen solid. I built a fire nearby to warm my hands as required. It was a tough skinning job, but I managed to get it done. Then I completely boned every ounce of meat off the carcass, filling up several game bags. Carrying the large, bulky bags over my shoulder like Santa Claus carries his bag of toys, I struggled to get them out to the cart. When all the bags were moved, I lashed on as many as I could, and then by myself got the cart back to the truck. This is basically a two person cart, but if you're careful enough, one person can actually manage it pretty well. At long last, I had all of my moose meat in the pickup before 4:00 in the afternoon.

It's funny how pain is soon forgotten once the discomfort is over and you're thinking about it a long ways down the road. As I write this, though, I can still remember how difficult it was to turn the key in the ignition, but I also remember how great the moose meat tasted. So you can bet that the next time I draw a moose tag, I'll probably do the whole thing over again. But it would be nice to have a companion along to help things out a little. To heck with hunting moose alone.

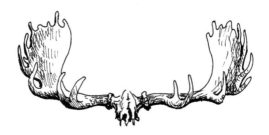

OKAY, I'LL SHOOT ONE ALONG THE ROAD

I was living in Vernal, Utah when I drew my first antelope tag. Believe me, I was really excited. It's interesting to look back on those early days. Now, after having lived in Wyoming so many years and seeing antelope as fairly easy quarry, it's hard to think back and feel that initial excitement. But any time I hunt an animal for the first time, I'm more excited than usual. If the time comes when I'm no longer excited, I'll give up hunting. I can't imagine that happening.

Utah isn't known as a top antelope state, so anyone who draws a tag there has really done something. I was pretty proud of myself for drawing that tag, and could hardly believe my good luck.

There are two ways to hunt antelope. The easy way and the hard way. The easy way, of course, is to road hunt. You merely drive down the road in the desert or prairie, spot an antelope, and then get out and shoot it (or shoot at it, as is often the case, depending on whether the animal is running or standing, how far away it is, and how good a shot you are.) Either way, road hunting was out for me. I said to heck with it.

I'd spent quite a bit of time in antelope country in Utah, and most of the animals I'd seen weren't exactly very wary. But I hadn't been around when they were being hunted, so I really didn't know what to expect. I wasn't anticipating a super smart quarry. I was soon to learn how wrong I was.

The area I hunted is the Bonanza unit, bordered on the east by Colorado, the White River to the south, and the Bookcliffs to the west. It is basically broken rimrock desert country with plenty of washes, greasewood bottoms, some pinion- juniper stands, and it is very, very arid. One particular place, called Kennedy Flat, seemed to hold most of the antelope.

Most of the people I talked to said the best way to hunt them was to simply drive out to Kennedy Flat and shoot one. Hunter success was very high, as it is in antelope units everywhere. I believe it was 85 or 90 percent. As I recall, there were maybe 30 or 40 tags for the entire unit. I was determined to do it the hard way, to shoot an antelope on foot. I was not going to spot one from the truck and shoot it.

One day, when I was scouting out the unit with a map, checking out the road system and looking for water holes, I happened to be stopped in one area looking at a map. Three doves flew across the greasewood, making a beeline up a small, rocky draw. I didn't think much of it, until a few minutes later a couple more doves also flew up into the draw. In the next 10 minutes, a half-dozen doves followed. It didn't take a rocket scientist to figure that there was a high likelihood of water in the draw. There were very few doves in that desert area, and they were never concentrated.

I hiked up the draw, and sure enough, I found a neat little waterhole tucked away in the bottom. It had been constructed for livestock, and it had plenty of water in an area that was extremely arid. Good news -- there were antelope tracks every-

Dan carries out his sleeping bag. We slept all night near the waterhole, waiting for opening morning.

where. This I believed, was going to be the place where I'd get my first antelope.

I did more scouting, checking out as much of the unit as possible. No other area looked as good as the waterhole. I was scouting remote spots away from roads, wanting to stay as far from other hunters as possible.

I was at the little waterhole long before shooting light on opening day with my 10-year old son, Dan. It was September, and though the early breeze had a chilly bite to it, I knew it was going to be very hot in the afternoon. I had hidden my truck about a half a mile away in a wash and was prepared to wait as long as was necessary.

As it turned out, nothing happened. No antelope showed at all. I forced myself to wait there until late in the afternoon, and then I couldn't stand it any longer. I'd have waited until dark, because antelope often go to water late in the day, but a number of hunters had driven down the road that was just 100 yards away. They couldn't see us, because we blended in well with the rimrock, and I figured they didn't know about the waterhole, but their presence could have alarmed any animals that were nearby. I felt that the human traffic might have been discouraging antelope from coming to water during daylight hours.

So much for our hotspot. I decided to try another area I'd found where I'd seen quite a few antelope tracks.

As Dan and I were driving down the road, I saw a cloud of dust far ahead. With my binoculars, I saw the butt ends of three or four antelope as they hastily sped away. We're talking real haste here. It's said that antelope can run 50 mph with the afterburners fired up; these critters were doing all of that and then some.

This behavior, as I quickly learned, was standard operating procedure for antelope after hunting season opened. The dumb antelope had been transformed into wily devils. Anytime a vehicle showed up they were on their feet and moving.

The next day I hunted, I decided to walk the length of a greasewood draw. The draws are dry washes with fine sand in the bottoms. I had a big canteen full of water, some fruit, and a couple sandwiches. Dan wasn't along, because he had something else going on in town.

It was not an eventful hike. I walked, and I walked, and never saw an antelope. The only live critters I saw that day were a couple horned lizards, several cottontails, and some Lbb's (little brown birds).

Mind you, this unit did not have a lot of antelope in it. From what I learned from locals, the only concentrations were in Kennedy Flat. With hunting season in full swing, the animals there were undoubtedly spooked and scattered, since that's where most hunters headed.

Antelope aren't always this trusting, most of the time they're off in a flash when you get too close.

As the days passed and I continued hiking the desert and rim-rock ridges to no avail, I began to appreciate the challenge of this hunt. I was still reluctant to simply shoot one from the vehicle. Invariably I'd see those telltale clouds of dust; I got to feeling the antelope were thumbing their noses at me.

I was having lots of luck on that hunt, all bad. I couldn't seem to find an animal within range. Occasionally I'd see a stationary buck at the outer limits of my self-imposed range, which was 400 yards. Even at that I'd be pushing it. When I did spot an animal too far out for a shot, I'd drive away, hide the truck, and sneak back. No good; Murphy's Law always prevailed.

My first antelope, the one I indeed shot next to the road.

The last day of the hunt arrived, and I was mighty frustrated. Negative, too. I was certain this wouldn't be any different than any of the other days of the hunt.

I decided to try a place I'd never been to before. It was close to the Colorado border and was an area that not very many people had talked about. Evidently there were few antelope in that spot, but I figured I couldn't do any worse by hunting there. Nothing else was clicking so far.

After checking my maps, I decided to drive out about a mile from the main road, park near the border, and just work my way along the rimrock ledges where I could see into the valleys below.

As it turned out, I didn't get that far. I was driving up a road and had to cross a very deep gully. I'd seen where a number of other vehicles had opted not to cross the gully and had turned around and gone back. This gully was a significant obstacle, even to a four-wheel drive rig. The little ATV's hadn't yet made the outdoor scene as they have today, so no one attempted to cross in a conventional vehicle.

Not to be defeated, I drove up along the four-foot deep gully and found a crossing, but I had to drive a half mile to do it. This was good. I realized that now I was perhaps in virgin country, where few, if any hunters had been to that season. Hopefully the gully had dissuaded other hunters.

As I was continuing on my way to the spot where I intended to park, I saw a bunch of antelope ahead and just a few yards off the road. They caught me totally by surprise. Was this for real? A bunch of honest-to-God antelope that weren't ripping along at Mach 1 speed, and close enough to hit with a slingshot? This was too much for my brain to comprehend. Perhaps the gray matter in my head was a bit fried from being in the sun so long.

What to do? Do I maintain my code of ethics because this buck was shootable from the road? Heck no. I earned this buck! Granted, he had itty bitty 12-inch horns, but they looked like two-footers to me.

As soon as I got out of the truck, they took off, trotting down a small gully. Great! They were now out of sight. I ran over a little rimrock ledge, and there they were, walking slowly. I rested the .30/06 on a big rock, drew a bead on the buck, and fired.

What do you know – my first antelope was in the bag. Believe me when I tell you I was a happy camper. Even though I hadn't hiked out to him in the middle of that vast desert, I had really worked hard for that critter, and I was plenty satisfied with the way it ended. I'm glad I said to heck with shooting one from the road, and I'm glad I changed my mind.

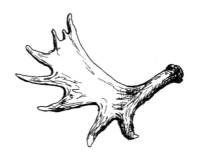

ARE YOU SURE
THE BLACK MAMBAS ARE ASLEEP?

*So...how the heck are we gonna' get
that in the freezer?*

Jack Atcheson's words were ringing in my ears as the jetliner touched down at the Johannesburg airport.

"Africa is like no place you've ever been to," he had told me. "It's a strange, mysterious land, a place that I can't describe. You'll have to go there to understand what I mean."

Jack's statement wasn't said in a matter of fact way. He spoke of Africa with a reverence, an eloquence that I hadn't seen coming from him before.

Atcheson, a well-known hunter's booking agent from Butte, Montana, had hunted Africa so many times he'd lost count. On many of those hunts he'd accompanied a number of writers, including Jack O'Connor and Jim Carmichel. My first recollections of Atcheson were of his hunts with O'Connor in the 60's. Since then, Atcheson and I had become close friends, and I was genuinely moved by his feelings about the Dark Continent. Maybe I should indeed go there to understand what he meant.

Fillamond, our tracker (center), joins Schalk and I as we pose with my blesbok. Schalk was a superb Professional Hunter, and Fillamond was also very skilled at reading sign and seeing game.

I'll confess that Africa hadn't been on my list of priorities. Though I hunt at least 130 days each year, I'd been content to roam North America. My hunts took me all over the U.S., to Canada and Alaska, and especially the Rockies where I live. I had no strong urge to go abroad, but I'll admit there was an increasing interest to finally go to Africa. I'd listened to too many stories from pals, and my job as Hunting Editor for OUT-DOOR LIFE continually nudged me along to seek new places. Atcheson's words were the final straw. I realized it was time to go. I'd said to heck with African hunting long enough.

Schalk Van Heerden clinched my decision. The 28-year old

professional hunter introduced himself to me at a Sportsman's Show in 1994 and described his operation. Explaining that he'd grown up on a large South African ranch that he'd been hunting on since he was eight, he came off as a competent and trustworthy young man. I felt comfortable with him at the outset. Africa, after all, would be a major adventure. And when a former client told me that Schalk could "follow a four-day old impala track across rocks," I was impressed. "Not only that," the client said, "you'll never find a harder working, more enthusiastic professional hunter than Schalk."

The die was cast. I was going to Africa.

My wife, Madonna, accompanied me, and she was as full of anticipation as I was. She'd go along as an observer.

Once the decision was made to go, we embarked on a trail of new discoveries – and concerns. What kinds of shots would we need? What would happen if we got hurt – are African blood supplies safe and Aids-free, and how about the Ebola virus outbreak in Zaire that was making daily headlines? And how about snakes? I'd heard plenty about black mambas and such.

This was camp. It was pampering at its best.

As it turned out, we needed to take only malaria pills, and have a tetanus shot. We quickly learned that South African medicine is amazingly modern – after all, didn't Dr. Christian Barnard, the man who made history with the first heart-transplant, perform his work in South Africa? As far as the terrifying Ebola outbreak was concerned, the virus was confined, in Zaire, and amounted to no concern, though practically every acquaintance worried for us. The snakes shouldn't be a problem, either, we were told. Our trip in June would be early winter in Africa, since their seasons are just the opposite of ours; with colder temperatures the snakes should be dormant.

And so it was that after a grueling 14-hour nonstop flight from New York, we arrived in South Africa, totally in awe at everything we saw. Simple questions such as the nature of the food, weather, customs, lifestyle and a myriad of others were quickly answered. In no time we were totally at ease in this brand new land. When you land in Johannesburg, one of South Africa's largest cities, you won't notice much difference from Cleveland, Buffalo, Indianapolis, or Atlanta. Joburg, as it's called locally, is a modern city. If it wasn't for the unfamiliar language, you'd think you were in the states.

When Schalk asked me how I preferred to hunt prior to our departure from the U.S., I told him I wanted to walk and still-hunt as much as possible. I'd heard a number of stories describing hunts from vehicles, and I wasn't interested. I wanted all of the adventure; tasting every aspect of the hunt and learning the habits of the species we'd pursue.

Schalk was eager to please, and, in fact, was an avid bowhunter. Every morning we stillhunted away from his hunting camp, slipping quietly through the thorny vegetation. Despite our stealth, we were unable to connect on a kudu, which is the premier plains game species in South Africa as well as many other African countries.

Stillhunting in Africa is something you don't read much about, and it was as challenging as any hunt I'd ever been on in the states. On several occasions an unseen kudu barked a warning, much as a cow elk. Blue wildebeests snorted at us from heavy cover, frustrating our efforts to get a clear shot. It took me five days of cat and mouse hunting to finally tag a wildebeest.

Hunting camp was really a chalet, a beautiful building complete with thatched roof. Our bedroom was on the top floor with an open bar beneath. Next door was Schalk's residence where we ate superb meals. This was pampering at its best. The bed sheets and clothing were laundered every day while we hunted. We returned to sparkling clean clothes and a spotless room.

Madonna and I with my gemsbok. This striking animal was one of our favorites.

The first animal I tried for was an impala, the ubiquitous animal that seems to live everywhere. Schalk had spotted a good one, and when I took a solid rest and fired, I was thinking the animal was history. Imagine my bewilderment when the impala took off running, seemingly unscathed.

We looked closely for blood, hair, anything to signify a hit, but it was evidently a clean miss. I was mighty upset, because I was shooting my pet Browning 7mm Rem Mag, and had just sighted it in hours before at Schalk's practice area. I couldn't explain the miss, especially since the impala had been standing still, 90 yards out.

Schalk solved the mystery. He pointed to a small sapling about one inch in diameter. It was neatly clipped in two by my bullet. Suffice to say I was relieved.

From that point on, by taking careful shots and using my shooting sticks, I took 11 animals with 11 shots. None of the quarry were running; all were standing broadside at ranges from 60 to 350 yards. Actually, I impressed the heck out of myself; I'd never before shot so accurately. I attributed my shooting to very intensive practice with the 7mm Mag. Prior to the hunt I used it frequently on prairie dogs, marmots, and jackrabbits.

A unique challenge, one you aren't confronted with in the U.S. (with the exception of mountain goats) is the need to identify males from females since the latter wear horns as well. With some African species, a female's horns may be longer. That being the case, I carefully evaluated each animal before taking the shot. A further complication was the difficulty in getting a clear shot. Contrary to what I'd read and heard, these African animals didn't stand around very long while you observed them. Many quickly ran into heavy cover when they detected our presence.

We hunted the northern Transvaal region, not far from the Botswana border. The area we hunted is known as the bushveld, a fairly flat to rolling terrain with vegetation that reminded me of south Texas. A good deal of the trees and bushes had thorns, so I learned to walk carefully, especially in the kudu woods.

One particular tree looked like a huge prickly pear cactus. It was 30-feet tall, and its sap contained a deadly toxin. Definitely not a user-friendly cactus as ours are. Another tree, called a tombuti, gives off poisonous fumes when its wood is burned. South Africans, who love to barbecue as much as they can, are careful to avoid the tombuti tree when cutting wood for their barbecue fires.

I'll admit I hardly knew a kudu from a kangaroo before the

trip. I had no idea of their size, their behavior patterns, or their intelligence.

It didn't take long to learn. Hunting a kudu on his own turf, afoot and sneaking along, is on a par with hunting a crafty mature whitetail buck. The kudu is an incredibly handsome animal, having long spiraling horns set atop a handsome head marked by a white chevron across the snout. He's big, weighing 600 pounds or more, and stands on long legs. Most importantly, those legs don't stand around very long when a human approaches too closely. The kudu will take instant flight or hide and slink about in heavy brush. Nightly wanderings keep the kudu out of trouble; he seldom ventures about during daylight hours.

I'm happy with my kudu, shown above with guide Neil Barnard. The kudu are one of the toughest species to hunt in Africa -- much like our whitetails.

This picture is out of focus because it's hard to be still when a rhinocerous or two is chasing you. Madonna took this photo.

This was my style of hunting, and when we looked for kudu in another area made up of koppies, or low rocky hills, I felt like I was back home. We sneaked along, and after topping out on a high ridge, we worked down to a low pass where we jumped a herd of kudu and I finally got a look at my first kudu bull. As luck would have it, the animal offered only a quick look as it tore along in the brush, but I was hooked on kudu hunting. One afternoon, Madonna and I and Neil Barnard, Schalk's guide, hiked through a wooded area hoping to ambush a kudu. Schalk's dad, Andres, had dropped us off in his vehicle, planning on picking us up a few miles away. Before departing, Andres talked to Neil in their Afrikaans language. I didn't understand, but I distinctly heard Andres mention the word "mamba". As we walked off through the brush, I asked Neil what Andres had said about snakes.

"He said there's lots of black mambas in this patch of woods, and to be careful," Neil replied. "But don't worry, we probably won't see any – it's the wrong time of the year."

Probably! That wasn't a very comfortable buffer.

We didn't see any black mambas, and no kudu either. This kudu hunt was reminding me of whitetails more and more. Trying to sneak up on a kudu in the koppie or in the woods was almost an impossibility. Loose rocks and a generous assortment of twigs and branches littered the hilly floor. Brush constantly snagged on clothing, putting everything within earshot at instant alert.

It took three more days before I saw another big kudu bull, but this time I was ready. While waiting in a makeshift ground blind with Madonna and Neil, the kudu showed up on a trail just before dark. It was his final walk.

Madonna relaxes in the courtyard behind camp.

I couldn't wait to see what the animal looked like close-up, and I wasn't disappointed. He was a lovely sight, with long, black 48-inch horns that spiraled three times.

We'd been hunting kudu only in the early morning and late afternoon, and pursued other species during the day.

Each time I approached an unfamiliar animal, I'll admit to a feeling of total amazement. These were species that I'd never seen before, except for a few at zoos, and I marveled at the sight of each one. I'd continually recall mounted heads I'd seen in the U.S., especially in Jack Atcheson's office and the taxidermy studio that bears his name. Suddenly the various animals became real. I could put names to them, as well as acquainting myself with the feel of their pelts and the unique designs of their horns.

I was impressed with the total consumption of the animals I'd taken. Not an ounce of flesh was wasted; carcasses were immediately hung in a large cooler after the kill. Even the head, feet, and all the entrails were eaten by the natives. The lower legs were tossed into a fire; when the hair was singed off, they were then parboiled and eaten.

When it was over, I came back with a new awareness. Africa wasn't such a Dark Continent after all, although I'll admit that we'd experienced some interesting incidents that wouldn't have occurred here at home. Like the three rhinos that trotted a bit too close to our Land Cruiser, making bluff charges. Or the puff adder's head that was barely two inches from Neil's hand when Neil picked up a branch to make way for our hunting vehicle. Or the fishing trip where it was suggested that we maintain a wary eye, since a croc's striking distance is easily 10 yards up from the shoreline -- or more, depending how fast you and the croc can run. Or the many times we thought about running into black mambas and hearing the famous saying: "If a black mamba bites you, walk to the closest shady tree and lie down. You should at least be comfortable during the last few minutes of your life." Or the wonderful relationship Madonna and I had established with African people; not only Schalk and his fiancee, Terina, but also Schalk's parents who run a large cattle ranch and were among the most hospitable folks I'd ever met.

Will I go back? You bet, because Schalk has a few 50 plus inch kudu I'd like to see again, as well as a few other species. As Jack Atcheson told me, "Once you go, you'll want to go back again and again. You can never get enough."

How right he is, and I'll never say to heck with African hunting again.

NOTE -- If you're interested in hunting South Africa, you can write to Schalk Van Heerden, Bush Africa Safaris, P.O. Box 375, Ellisras 0555, South Africa, or call (011) 27-14-7634549.

SIR JACK,
MAY I PLEASE
SHOOT THAT
RAM?

The rock under my foot suddenly gave way with no warning. Grabbing wildly at a bush, I managed to stop my fall just in time. I wiped sweat from my forehead and continued easing down the rocky slope, thankful I wore hunting boots which offered a secure grip, if there IS such a thing on that unbelievably steep boulder-strewn sidehill. With some optimism, I noted that the two rams were only a half mile away. That knowledge offered the necessary motivation to continue along the treacherous slopes.

The terrain was awesome. Rocks ranging in size from footballs to bathtubs were arranged in a loose formation, requiring intense concentration. You didn't plunge your weight on a rock – you gingerly tested it first.

Sheep country can be unforgiving. It's not a place that allows mistakes, especially in the upper reaches where your life may depend on a precarious foothold or the strength of a skinny branch. Losing your balance is not an option.

Jack Atcheson, Jr. and I had initially spotted the pair of rams more than a mile and a half away. It was barely light enough to see, and we estimated it would take nearly half a day to get within shooting range if the rams were indeed worthy of a closer look. Atcheson made the decision to move in with no hesitation.

I had no doubts as to my guide's ability to judge sheep. Jack Atcheson Jr., commonly known as "Junior", is believed by many hunters, including me, to be the top sheep hunter in North America. That's why I agreed to take him on as a hunting companion. When he was in his early 20's, Jack had completed the revered Grand Slam, taking all four subspecies of sheep in North America. He commonly guides hunters who are high bidders for auctioned Governor's tags, and he recently discovered the remains of the biggest ram to have lived in the U.S. Jack Jr. is to sheep hunting as Joe Montana is to football.

Ask me what is the toughest hunt in the lower 48, and I'll tell you with no hesitation that it's the unlimited sheep hunt in Montana. By "unlimited", I'm referring to several units that do not require a lottery draw for a tag. No other state offers such tags.

But there's a catch – actually several catches. Though anyone can buy a permit across the counter for these units, there's a very low quota, typically less than half a dozen for each unit. In other words, if a unit has a quota of three tags, the hunt ends when three rams are taken.

That's the easy catch. The tough one? If you opt to hunt this country, you're looking at some of the most rugged, remote, grizzly-infested terrain in the Rockies. Many areas have no trails; if they do, they're foot trails. You'd be a fool to take a horse into much of that region. This boils down to foot hunting – carrying all your gear on your back, sleeping where and when you can, and hoping you'll see a fresh sheep track soon, maybe in another day or two.

Not many hunters can endure the hardship of this hunt for more than a few days. Most go in enthused, assuming they're in great shape, but come out prematurely – whipped and much wiser to the realities of this hunt. I know seasoned outfitters who have tried this hunt on their own, hoping for a ram for their lodge wall. Most come out defeated, swearing they'll never go back.

One man stands out who beats the dismal odds in these god-forsaken units – who invariably gets his client into a ram – provided the client can meet the awesome physical challenge. You guessed it. Jack Jr. does it.

Jack had tried to call me several times when he learned I'd drawn a tag. So did several other people. Since I was in Africa at the time of the drawing; I had no idea of my incredibly good luck until two weeks afterward. In fact, the permit was buried in a huge pile of mail when I got home. It took another three days to learn of its presence.

Drawing a sheep tag in Montana is like hitting a publisher's sweepstakes contest. I'd been applying for 15 years and never expected to draw. Being awarded a hunting tag anywhere has been tough. I'm not lucky, but through persistence I've managed to pick up a tag here and there. The Montana sheep tag was the ultimate. This was to be the hunt of a lifetime.

I'm not a newcomer to sheep hunting, having hunted in other states, including a backcountry adventure in the famous Thoroughfare country near Cody, Wyoming where I live. That hunt, with outfitter Nate Vance, was everything a sheep hunt could be, from stalks through snow-capped peaks to eating sheep ribs over a campfire.

In reality, no state can begin to match Montana's giant rams. People there speak of 190 and 195 sheep as if they were everyday occurrences – which they are. But why? What's the reason for the giant rams in the Big Sky state? Wildlife professor Gene

Decker of Colorado State University believes it's simply a matter of nutrition – nothing more. That's an unpopular opinion in
most hunting circles, since most sheep hunters would have you
believe that there's a unique gene in Montana's herds that produce enormous horns.

"Not so," says Dr. Decker. "Montana's sheep have high quality food. Nutrition means everything."

The unit I drew has a good bit of public land. Locating sheep
from the many roads within isn't difficult, but spotting a truly
huge ram and identifying it as such, takes some doing. And, as
I soon found out, so does negotiating the miserable terrain. Just
because you can see a ram from your vehicle doesn't mean you
can easily get to it.

Though I'd been around big rams before, this unit was special, abounding in rams so huge that dozens would easily make
the Boone and Crockett record book. Being fooled by large rams
is easy, because when they reach maturity they all look big. The
exceptional ram may be just around a ledge, and in many cases
Mr. Big shows up when a hunter drops a lesser animal. That's
why I wanted Jack along. He knows a great ram from a REAL-
LY great ram.

We based out of outfitter Ed Josephson's lodge near
Thompson Falls, which was fairly close to our unit. Sleeping
between sheets and showering regularly seemed peculiar. Sheep
hunting normally means sleeping bags and campfire-cooked
food. Atcheson was amused when I commented on the unusual
lodging.

"This is the most amazing sheep hunt you'll ever experience,"
he said. "Not at all in traditional style, but wait until you see the
monster rams. The toughest part of the hunt was drawing the
tag. Now it's a matter of lots of glassing and locating the ram we
want."

The season had already been open a week when we headed
out, since Jack had had a long time commitment to guide another sheep hunter. I'll admit I was anxious, but not worried. The
season still had two more months to go.

Of course, I could have headed over to the unit and hunted
opening week without Jack. I was tempted to do so many times,
but I always had the nagging feeling that Murphy's Law would

The dream of a lifetime – a really good bighorn sheep.

prevail. For me, Murphy can show up at any moment. I could picture myself tagging a ram that would be a boomer around home in Wyoming, but hardly an eye-opener in Montana. I see "good" rams around my house eight months out of the year, and drool when I photograph a rare 180 sheep. Not good enough on this hunt. I know me and I know I'd be tempted to take the first decent ram that showed up. Nope, ol' buddy Jack would be calling the shot.

Our first hike was through a recently burned forest. Stopping to glass from high overlooks, we saw several rams feeding about, but only one appeared promising. He fed on a mountainside across a big draw. The ram seemed to be alone, and his horns looked very long. After more glassing, Jack wanted another look from a better position. I could sense that this ram might be questionable to Jack, though he looked super dandy to me.

The ram was in a hidden pocket, unseen from most locations except the original one where we'd first spotted him. He wasn't far from a road, and if it wasn't for the lay of the land, another hunter likely would have seen him. The sheep would have been taken to someone's taxidermist real quick.

After more glassing, Jack thought best to leave this ram for a while. Left to me, I'd have shot the ram in a heartbeat. The horns were quite long, but not enough mass in Jack's way of thinking.

"That ram will fool you," he said. "I like the horn length, but his bases aren't great. I'll bet he barely makes 180. We can do a whole lot better."

So who was I to argue with the master? Off the mountain we came, and I started seriously questioning my sanity.

That wasn't the end of it for the day, either. Later on that afternoon we saw six more rams; at least three were record-book status. And again Atcheson gave the thumbs down sign. He grinned as he did so, because I was in a semi-state of shock, disbelieving what we were seeing and what I was doing. Or NOT doing.

I must confess that we spotted several more sheep while pumping gas in Plains, Montana. That's right – you read it correctly. The rams were cavorting on a mountainside just above the schoolhouse. It was unbelievable to see those animals literally in town. I didn't mention this observation in my articles on the hunt because I didn't want to draw national attention to these easily accessible sheep.

The next morning we spotted the pair of rams that I already mentioned. With the sun barely clearing the eastern horizon, we headed around the rim to a point where we could drop down on the sheep. Working along the ridge wasn't tough, but I wasn't looking forward to the inevitable descent, down to where we last saw the rams.

Jack couldn't stand it. He measured the ram's bases with his belt, then compared it to a six-inch dollar bill.

It was worse than I thought. Moving slowly, I eased my way downward, trying to keep noise to a minimum, which was practically impossible. Rocks clattered underfoot at almost every step. Worse, the wind changed to the sheep's advantage, provided they were still in the general area.

Jack Jr. carries about 130 pounds off the mountain. I had about 80 pounds on my back. (Jack is younger than me.)

We sat down, awaiting a change in the wind, but only after we tried to make a big circle. No use. The slope was even steeper; we'd need ropes to lower ourselves down.

The wind swapped around a half hour later, giving us the break we needed. Immediately we continued the descent, now cautiously looking for the rams.

In my mind I had this scenario figured out: Jack would spot the rams, set up the spotting scope, and carefully evaluate the larger animal. If he gave me the green light, I'd ease into prone position, take a solid rest, and shoot the sheep from a relaxed, comfortable position.

It didn't work out that way. Not even close.

The rams erupted from their beds and ran into a small group of trees where they stopped for a moment to look at us. Evidently they'd heard us but hadn't yet spotted us.

There was absolutely no indecision in Jack's mind; in fact he never raised his binoculars.

"Shoot!" he exclaimed. "Shoot!"

But I had a major problem. The smaller ram was standing on the far side of the giant. Chances of my bullet passing through one ram and hitting the other were too good. I was poised, ready for the rams to make a move, and I'll confess that my nerves weren't exactly in fine form.

Suddenly the sheep took off and ran through the rocks, still abreast of each other. I held my fire, waiting for the opportunity I needed, and it finally came when the big ram moved well up in front of the smaller sheep. They were just about to crest a ridgetop when I fired.

The great ram was on the ground, and I bent down on one knee, covering it to make sure it didn't get up. The sheep showed no movement. It was then that I realized my usually calm mentor was sprinting full bore toward the fallen ram. I ran right behind him, but took a flying leap when a rock rolled. Luckily, I skid to a quick stop in the treacherous rockslide. Moving at a little slower pace, I crossed the distance and went on over to the ram.

It was over. I had no doubts that the finest sheep I'll ever see in my lifetime was lying before my feet. Curiously, I had no interest in its score at that point. Somehow ranking numbers would have taken something away from the emotion of the moment. I wanted to enjoy the sheep for what he meant to me, rather than whether or not he stacked up to modern man's standards. Don't get me wrong. I was looking forward to having the sheep eventually scored, and the score would be a conversation piece the rest of my life. But right then I didn't care.

"I forgot my measuring tape," Jack said as he rummaged through his huge pack." I can't believe it. I always carry that tape."

"Good!," I said. "Right now let's not worry about it." (The ram ended up scoring 187 Boone and Crockett; minimum score to make the book is 180. He would have easily made 190, but at least three inches were lost because of two big chunks in his horn – each where a measurement must be taken. The sheep took an Honorable Mention award at the annual convention hosted by the Foundation For North American Wild Sheep.)

On any hunt involving rough country, elation soon fades to reality. Getting the sheep out would be an ordeal. Jack, who is a former taxidermist, skinned the animal while I removed quarters and boned them. With the meat, hide, and horns, we began the precarious descent with extremely heavy loads. I estimated Jack had 130 pounds on his back; I carried about 80.

Being determined to eat sheep ribs intact, I couldn't fit them in the packs, so I carried them in my hand, while at the same time easing off the mountain with a stout walking stick. Unable to get the meat, horns, and hide to the vehicle that day, we cached them high in a tree to thwart the numerous black bears that inhabited the area. It was a long hike back up the mountain to the truck that night, and another long haul in the morning to bring out the sheep.

Our log home in Wyoming's mountains has an empty spot on the loft overlooking the living room. When we built the house a few years ago, I asked my wife's opinion of what to do with that empty area.

"Let's wait until you get a big ram," she said, "We can have it mounted life-size; it'll fit perfectly up there."

"But I may never get another decent sheep," I argued.

"Sure you will," she responded. "Just you wait and see."

I hate it when your wife is always right. In this case, however, I was glad mine was.

BARB – DON'T HAVE YOUR BABY
ON THE PRAIRIE

Bill Brown carefully lifted the hot lid of the Dutch oven and peered inside. A savory aroma immediately drifted across our campsite, whetting already hungry appetites. We ate soon afterward, and relaxed in the little Wyoming valley rimmed with ledges and rocky outcrops.

As if on cue, a coyote barked sharply as we sipped pleasant libations after the hearty meal. It was a nice ending to a good day, but I couldn't wait for night to end. Dawn would bring with it opening morning of the 1983 antelope season in our unit, and I had plenty of reason to be excited. Our scouting efforts turned up so many antelope I couldn't decide where to hunt first. I was familiar with the area, having hunted it for prong-horns every year for the last seven years. But this season seemed different. It was almost impossible to glass a sagebrush flat or rolling prairie and not see a good antelope buck. In some places more than a hundred antelope could be observed from a single vantage point.

"We've got antelope coming out of our ears," Bill Brown said as he stirred the ashes in the campfire. "This year's harvest should be the best on the record."

Bill Brown should know. At the time, he was information manager for the Wyoming Game and Fish Department, and he was plenty optimistic about antelope. So were the rest of us. Our party consisted of Bill and his wife, Lynda, and daughter, Devlin, Craig and Barb Leerberg, Bruce Huibregths, and Bob Chalstrom. Bill and his family were along just for a bit of rest and relaxation, but the rest of us were primed for prong-horns—big bucks that roamed this part of Wyoming.

We were ready long before dawn. I slept fitfully in my small mountain tent, thinking about a particular place I'd watched the day before. It was my favorite spot, one in which I had killed several antelope over years past, and one that commonly pro-duces a few 15-inch bucks as well as an occasional 16-incher every year. According to most antelope standards, those are dandy bucks anywhere in pronghorn country. The problem was, however, that I'd seen plenty of good bucks in other areas as well. I wasn't sure where to start in the morning.

I mentioned my plight while sipping hot black coffee around the cookstove just before we left camp.

"A real dilemma you have, Zumbo," Bill Brown chuckled. "How many hunters would love to have such problems. So much game out there you don't know where to begin hunting!"

Bill was right. Every once in a while it's nice to hunt game country so superb you don't worry about seeing game—just tying your tag to an exceptional trophy.

Craig, Barb, and I headed out together and decided to try my traditional spot. It was a steep sidehill covered with waist-high sagebrush, rocky outcroppings, and a stand of limber pines and junipers on top of the ridge. I liked the area because it held lots of antelope, but more importantly, it offered good stalking opportunities. Several small draws and dips on the slope allowed sneak and ambush tactics. I don't like to make long-range shots at pronghorns as many other hunters do, preferring instead to crawl within 100 yards or so. Another technique I like is to take cover in a clump of sage and wait for a herd of antelope to work their way within good shooting range. I'd used both methods successfully on this slope.

Part of hunting is sitting around the fire, enjoying your companions and the great outdoors. We're doing that here.

This was a very special hunt for Barb. She was eight months pregnant, and in high spirits. I suspect Craig was a bit nervous about his wife's condition, but she wasn't about to take things easy. Barb was ready for whatever the hunt would dish out –within reason, of course.

Craig parked his 4WD a half-mile from the hunting area and we split up to hunt on our own. Barb is an accomplished hunter, and hoped to tag a good buck. She was prepared to pass up several pronghorns for the one she wanted.

I picked my way cautiously through the sagebrush and clumps of cactus. Shooting light was still 20 minutes away, and I didn't want to spook antelope in the area. Mule deer also lived on the mountain, and would alert antelope if I blundered into a herd of deer and put them to flight.

By the time shooting light appeared, I was close to a small rim that shielded me from a little flat which always held antelope. I peeked over the top, and wasn't disappointed. At least 75 pronghorns were grazing in the new light, including a half-dozen shootable bucks. All were in the 14-inch class, and one looked as if it might go to 15.

If I wanted to, I could have found a comfortable rest for my Winchester .30/06 and made an easy 125 yard shot at one of the bucks. I opted to pass up the shot because it was opening morning and there were plenty of antelope to look at yet. The biggest buck in the herd was farther away than I cared to shoot, and there were too many animals to try a stalk. All those eyes out there would do me in before I got 10 yards on my belly.

I backed away from the rim and headed up the mountain to make a circle around the herd without spooking them. A bigger buck might be just out of sight over the next ridge. I moved carefully, but hadn't gone 20 yards when I heard an antelope snort at me. I looked over to see a small herd of a dozen does and a 12-inch buck scrambling down the mountain. I had blundered into them as they fed unseen in a small draw.

The antelope ran into the bigger herd and started them moving as well. I continued around the mountain, and 10 minutes later was glassing three separate herds, all containing respectable bucks, but nothing that interested me.

The rest of the morning produced the same results. By the time I got back to the vehicle for lunch I figured I'd counted more that 300 antelope.

Craig and Barb reported the same story. Craig made a stalk on a fine buck, one he judged to be 15 inches or better, but other antelope in the area stymied his approach and he wasn't able to

Lacking a tree branch, I hang my antelope from a quickly-made tripod and skin it next to camp.

close the distance for a good shot. Barb watched several dozen antelope walk by her position, including some good bucks, but she wasn't ready to make a choice yet.

After lunch we decided to try another area. The country we hunted was largely owned by ranchers, but there was some public land administered by the U.S. Bureau of Land Management as well. Two ranchers owned most of the land, and they gave us permission to hunt. The large numbers of antelope were making serious inroads on cattle forage, and ranchers depended on hunters to keep pronghorns thinned.

There were other hunters in the unit, but competition wasn't keen. Most of the time it was possible to stalk a herd of antelope with no disturbance from other hunters. This is the case over much of Wyoming, except for units located close to urban areas.

Our afternoon hunt was unproductive, though I was tempted to try for a buck with thick bases and long horns that curved inward at the tips. He wasn't exceptional, probably about 14 inches, but he was pretty.

Judging an antelope's measurements is never easy. Horns with thick bases and long prongs are immediately apparent, giving a false impression as to length. I've seen experienced hunters shoot bucks with massive horns, figuring them to be easily 14 or 15 inches, only to find they were barely 13 inches. Then again, I've seen 15 inch horns that were so thin they were hardly impressive. As in everything else, a trophy is in the eyes of the beholder.

After another culinary delight prepared by Bill's Dutch oven, we discussed the large numbers of antelope we'd seen. Bill said the Wyoming Game and Fish Department had 102,000 antelope permits for sale, a record number. About 10,000 of these went unsold that year.

This was an interesting development in light of the disastrous 1978-79 winter that left thousands of antelope dead all over Wyoming and much of the west. According to wildlife officials, almost 100 percent of the hardest-hit herds were wiped out. However, antelope have the ability to recover and quickly re-occupy barren environments. Obviously, we were seeing the results of that swift recovery.

The following day was eventful for four of us. Craig, Barb,

Bob and I tied our tags on respectable bucks. No exceptional trophies, just good above-average bucks. I had a commitment elsewhere and couldn't hold out for a bigger buck, and Craig and Barb wanted to hunt sage grouse. Bruce was prepared to stay another day or two to find the buck he wanted.

Hunter success on antelope in Wyoming is usually 90 percent and better. I suspect the people who don't score either make only a token effort or don't hunt at all.

Of all the big game in the West, antelope are the easiest to hunt, especially during years with record numbers of pronghorns on the prairies. A do-it-yourself hunt is practical and economical, allowing you to design your hunt according to your needs. You can base out of a motel and hunt comfortably each day, or you can camp right out in antelope country with a tent or camp unit. If the weather is good, you can sleep under the stars. Some ranchers take in hunters and provide room and board as well as private land to hunt on. Many outfitters in antelope states will give you guide service, sleeping facilities, and care of your animal once it's down.

Figure at least three days if you're serious about antelope hunting, and five or more if you're indeed seeking an enormous buck. If you want a representative buck, you should be able to do so in a day or so in the better units.

If you've never hunted antelope before or have only a season or two under your belt, it's wise to hire a guide or outfitter or at least hunt with someone experienced in pronghorn hunting if you want a bragging-size buck. As I mentioned, it's tough to judge a buck, and you might be disappointed if the so-called 15 incher you centered in your scope turns into a 13 incher.

In the event you're planning on hunting public land with a buddy or two, write for maps of the region you want to hunt. Since the Bureau of Land Management controls most public antelope range, write the agency at the appropriate state office. If you want to hunt national forests, write for maps at the supervisor's office of the particular forest you want to hunt.

Be aware that some states do not require landowners to post their property. It's up to the hunter to determine where he or she is. A good map is necessary, and it's a good idea to inquire locally as well. Much private land is unfenced and looks identical to public rangeland.

Chances are good your hunt will take place during hot days. For quality meat, skin your antelope immediately and chill the carcass promptly. There are a number of meat plants in the West where you can trade in your antelope meat and purchase an equal amount of already processed sausages and salamis. Most years I bone my antelope at camp and have the meat professionally processed.

Craig and Barb, who was eight months pregnant, pose with Barb's antelope. I'm glad she didn't have her baby there!

If you've ever been around antelope, you'll note a strong odor as you approach the animal. The smell will disappear as soon as you skin the carcass. Antelope often have a reputation of being "gamey" in the gastronomic department, but I suspect the animal wasn't cooled quickly enough after it was shot.

Few people say to heck with antelope hunting. The critters are plentiful, easy to see, and hunting success is usually very high. Besides, the beauty, smells and sounds of the prairie are unique and not easily forgotten. That's plenty of reason to head for antelope country again and again.

There's a nice sequel to this story. About 10 years after this hunt, Craig and Barb visited the International Sportsman's Expo in Denver where I was giving seminars on big game hunting. I hadn't seen them in years, which is why I didn't recognize the lovely nine year old girl with them.

Barb smiled warmly when she introduced me to the youngster who she'd been carrying while on our hunt.

"She hunts, too, Jim," Barb said. "She got several pheasants on a hunt last fall."

I couldn't resist the opportunity to introduce the young lady at my next seminar that afternoon. As it turned out, my slide program had a picture of Craig and Barb posing with Barb's antelope. The slide easily depicted Barb's maternal condition. While the slide was being shown on the screen, I asked the young hunter to come up on the stage, whereupon I acquainted her with the audience. As expected, the applause was genuine and hearty. That seminar was one of my most memorable.

THE BOAR THAT WANTED REVENGE

Did yea get that on film?

The Alabama forest had some nasty thickets, dense enough to hide a bunch of wild boars. It was the thought of those animals that brought me to the area in the first place. With some luck, my pal and I would be eating pork sausage when the hunt was over.

I never realized when I walked into those southern woods, however, that in a couple hours I'd be witnessing one of the most frightening scenes I'd ever experienced in 35 years of hunting.

This wasn't my first wild boar hunt, but it was by far the most unique. In the past, I'd made pig hunts in California, Florida, and Texas.

The California hunts were done by spotting and stalking, and I managed to take an animal on each of two hunts. The first boar sprinted out of a burned-out redwood stump, only after I practically stepped on it to make it flush. I had no idea the animal was hiding close by, and I managed to compose myself and fire at it on the run. The .30/06 bullet hit him solidly, and my first pig was down.

The next year I took a California boar after spotting him about 300 yards away. I was able to move a bit closer, and anchored him at 250 yards.

In Florida, I hunted boars after taking a turkey on a spring hunt with Lovett Williams, who manages a splendid lodge at Fish Eating Creek. I saw a number of pigs, but I was looking for the boss boar of the valley. I didn't see him, so I opted to go home with only a turkey.

My Texas boar hunts were incidental to whitetail deer hunting, and I've taken a number of pigs from the Lone Star State. I never turn down the opportunity to shoot a pig if it's allowed by the landowner. Given my druthers, I'll shoot a medium-sized sow, since I'm more interested in the meat than in the size of the tusks. Some big old boars are practically inedible, even when made into powerfully spiced sausage.

The biggest boar I'd ever seen was a giant pig in Texas. While driving back to hunting camp with my good buddy Gary Roberson, who owns Burnham Brothers Calls, Gary spotted a pig feeding alongside the road. In a flash, Gary hit the brakes, grabbed his rifle, piled out of the truck, and shot the boar. The tusks were absolutely unbelievable. They were thick, sharp, and several inches long. Having been raised on a Texas ranch where wild boars were common, Gary announced he'd never seen a bigger pig. It was all we could do to lift it into the vehicle. I have no idea what it weighed, but it was several hundred pounds.

But back to the Alabama hunt. It was during the winter of 1991 when my good buddy John Phillips suggested we hunt boars in Alabama after a January deer hunt. It seemed like a good idea when John proposed it, especially when he suggested we try hunting pigs with black-powder handguns. I'd never used a handgun of that type before, though I'd done a good bit of hunting with black-powder rifles and conventional revolvers.

The primitive handgun hunt would offer a new opportunity, and I was more than mildly curious to give the firearm a try. I met John at his Alabama home in late January, and we drove a couple hours south to the hunting area.

Dennis Smith, who produces outdoor TV shows in the South, accompanied us on the hunt. John and I were to be on camera, which meant we needed to find a cooperative wild boar.

(Photo by John Phillips)

I practice shooting with the black-powder revolver before heading out to hunt pigs.

We were based at Osage Orange Hunting Lodge perched on a small hill near Greensboro, Alabama. I was quickly impressed, because we'd be treated to home-cooked meals, and the lodge was comfortable. I'd been on the road several weeks doing hunting seminars in the West, and I was tired of restaurant food and hotels. The lodge and the hunt offered an opportunity to relax, and I'm a big fan of southern cooking, which made the hunt even more attractive. It was nice not to have to deal with any business pressures or timetables. The only pressure we had was to find a wild boar or two.

To help meet that objective, we used a dog owned by Searce (pronounced Sir-see) Averett, who manages the lovely lodge. The dog, named Cookie, was not exactly the fierce boar-hunting hound I'd expected on such a hunt. Cookie was a cross between a border collie and something else, and I'll admit I had some misgivings when the dog followed us out of the lodge. It was a small canine, mincing along lightly on the ground, instead of plodding about with nose to the ground and fire in its eyes, as most hounds would be expected to do.

Before heading out, we thoroughly practiced shooting the CVA (Connecticut Valley Arms) revolvers. At first, we loaded only one cylinder and fired it; then we loaded all five and fired them rapidly. We left one cylinder empty for safety purposes. When the gun was loaded, the hammer was always positioned over the empty cylinder.

Our initial efforts were aimed at becoming familiar with loading and firing the revolvers. With that accomplished, we spent a good deal of time punching round balls through a paper target at various distances. When we stepped into the woods, we wanted to know exactly how the guns would perform.

After a short ride in the vehicles, we arrived at the hunting area. The woods were a mix of hardwood and softwood trees, with some swampy spots and areas of very dense underbrush. Searce claimed it was a great spot to hunt boars, and I believed him. I was new at this, and had no idea what good boar country in Alabama was supposed to look like.

We had been walking through the southern forest for about an hour when the little dog began barking. Heading in her direction, we worked our way through dense stands of brush combined with reasonably open hardwood forest. According to Searce, most of the boars would be in the thick cover.

John and I decided we'd take turns. Whenever the dog bayed a pig, one of us would sneak in for the shot. If the pig broke away, the other hunter would make the next attempt, and so on.

I won the first flip, so I worked my way toward the dog with Searce, while John and Dennis followed close behind.

As we neared Cookie, I couldn't see the boar, but Searce told me the dog would be within seven or eight feet of it. Try as I might, I couldn't make the pig out in the shaded underbrush, so I carefully eased closer.

Finally I saw a dark shape just behind a log. Searce, who was directly behind me, confirmed my suspicions. The boar was the dark spot, but the log shielded part of his body. Nonetheless, I had room for a chest shot, but it had to be precise.

I found the best position I could, and found a steady rest for the handgun. The shot would be about 20 yards.

The ball was on its mark, but what I thought was the boar was really a dark part of the log. The pig flushed from its hiding place when the ball thudded into the log, and the little dog took up the chase.

For the next hour, we pursued Cookie and the boar, but every time we caught up to the bayed boar, it took off. This was a smart pig, obviously realizing that our presence meant more danger than the dog.

At one point Cookie had the pig cornered in high, thick grass. It was John's turn, and he slipped up carefully.

This time it appeared that the boar would allow a close approach, but it suddenly exploded from the vegetation. John fired at the escaping boar, hitting it solidly, but the animal continued to run.

John ran after the pig, and fired again. The ball again hit the boar, but the animal still didn't go down. What happened next will forever be etched in my memory.

John tripped as he ran, falling hard to the ground. The boar spun instantly, charging straight for John, who was lying prone in the weeds. With no chance to get up, John fired at the rushing boar. Still the pig came, this time within a few yards of John.

With the advancing pig charging straight at him, John shot again, this time hitting the boar in the head. The animal spun and fell to the ground dead. From where John was lying, he could have reached out and touched the dead boar with a five-foot stick.

It was over. John had barely escaped serious injury, and I learned firsthand that wild boars indeed can be dangerous quarry.

Dennis and I were about 40 yards from John when the incident occurred. We saw every bit of the drama unfold, and were helpless to do anything about it because it had happened so quickly. I doubt if the incident lasted more than five seconds.

When we walked over to John, we discussed the fact that he was lucky to be in one piece. John was delighted at the way the episode ended, and indicated he wasn't much interested in being involved in any more wild boar charges.

John Phillips with the wild boar that almost caused him major problems.

As we discussed the near tragedy, we realized we had completely forgotten about the fact we were to have been on film. Dennis' cameraman appeared a few minutes after the excitement was over, having no idea what he'd missed. Dennis lamented the fact that he could have had an unbelievable, honest wild boar attack on film, but that wasn't meant to be.

Dennis wasn't interested in getting a kill on film, so it wasn't required that the cameraman follow us around. Nonetheless, it was the chance of a lifetime - a video photographer's dream. As it turned out, only John, Dennis and I would be able to recount the memory; Murphy's law once again. I'm not even sure that John wants to remember it at all. For sure, John said to heck with that pig, and to heck with Murphy too!

Boots R. Reynolds

A lot has been said about Boots Reynolds, but most of it can't be printed. One printable comment was made, however, by a friend, who said, "He can buck a fella off harder with a paintbrush than any bronc I've ever seen!" Maybe that's because Boots has been down lookin' up enough times himself.

Boots is really Roy Reynolds, who was born and raised on the ranches of the Osage country of Oklahoma. It was on these ranches that he got his education as a cowboy. He's been on, over, under and around horses all his life and his career began at the age of eight as a brush track jockey riding matched races in Oklahoma. In the early 70's, Boots ended up in northern Idaho where he now resides with his wife, Becky, and where he devotes himself full-time to drawing and painting.

Always seeing humor in his surroundings it was just a matter of time until his drawings became cartoons. After years of drawing these 'funny pictures" for friends and family he decided to try his hand at sharing them with the public. Somebody, somewhere, must have liked them as his pen and ink cartoons have appeared in such magazines as Western Horseman, Horseman, ProRodeo Sports News, Horse and Horseman, and Horse and Rider.

Somehow, despite the demand and popularity of his artwork, Boots has managed to find some spare pieces to hang in a few galleries. (Rumor has it that he pays them to hang his paintings.) He now has his work displayed in galleries in Issaquah, Washington, Coeur d'Alene, Idaho and Cody, Wyoming.

According to Boots, "I think the western art world and the public are ready for something a little different and the way things are going in the world we could all use a little more humor and I plan to give it to them. They can laugh at my stuff all they want to."

Boots' artwork, including originals and prints may be purchased through Guildhall Publishing, 3505 N. West Loop 820, Fort Worth, TX 76106, or call 1-800-356-6733.

Books By Jim Zumbo

Finally, the books, videos and cassettes by one of the country's most widely known and respected outdoor writers, Jim Zumbo, Hunting Editor of Outdoor Life, are available by direct mail.

You've read his stories in Outdoor Life, American Hunter, and many other magazines. Now you can have his autographed books for your very own collection.

ALL BOOKS WILL BE AUTOGRAPHED!

ORDER TODAY
CALL 1-800-673-4868, (307) 587-5486

OR SEND YOUR REQUEST AND PAYMENT TO
WAPITI VALLEY PUBLISHING COMPANY
P.O. Box 2390, Cody, WY 82414

AMAZING VENISON RECIPES
FINALLY -- NEVER FRET ABOUT GAMEY VENISON AGAIN!

200 extraordinary recipes for deer, elk, moose, and other big game. Illustrated with chapters for beginning cooks, foolproof recipes for the gamiest meat, busy day recipes, information on field care, aging, marinades, and more. Comb bound. 232 pages. ISBN 0-9624025-4-0. **$16.95 plus $4.00 shipping and handling.**

"With 200 recipes, advice for beginners, and tips on field care, cutting, wrapping, and freezing, this book deserves a place in every hunter's kitchen."
                                                        - American Hunter

Books By Jim Zumbo

TO HECK WITH ELK HUNTING

This book recounts 30 of Jim's favorite hunting tales. Most are humorous, but some are bizarre. You'll laugh a lot when you read Jim's confessions of the elk woods, but you'll learn plenty, too. Illustrated with Jim's photos and hilarious cartoons drawn by famed cowboy humor artist, Boots Reynolds. Hardcover. 186 pages. ISBN 0-9624025-2-4. **$17.95 plus $4.00 shipping and handling.**

TO HECK WITH DEER HUNTING

Packed with tales of deer hunts around the continent, from Canada to Mexico; New York to Washington. Humorous tales of several dozen hunts, of which about half are whitetails; the others about muleys and blacktails. Jim truthfully tells the stories exactly as they happened. You'll learn about deer hunting too, as he recounts his mistakes as well as his successes. Illustrated by Boots Reynolds and Jim's photos. Hardcover. 188 pages. ISBN 0-9624025-3-2. **$17.95 plus $4.00 shipping and handling.**

HUNTING AMERICA'S MULE DEER

Accelerated hunting pressure and increased access to hinterlands have created a new breed of mule deer -- not in a biological sense, of course, but in terms of behavior. Muleys have become increasingly wary. There are still plenty of big bucks out there, but few are easily taken. This is the first book ever done on every phase of mule deer hunting, and is now a classic. Zumbo discusses the best ways to hunt them -- how, when, and where to hunt all seven subspecies, from the Rocky Mountain and desert varieties to the blacktails. Plenty of photos, with valuable information on trophy hunting. Acclaimed to be the best on the subject. Hardcover. 360 pages. ISBN 0-9624025-1-6. **$19.95 plus $4.00 shipping and handling.**

Books By Jim Zumbo

CALLING ALL ELK

The only book on the subject of elk hunting that covers every aspect of elk vocalization. Jim calls on all his experiences to share his expertise with the reader. This book differs from others because it deals with elk hunting throughout the entire fall instead of just the bugling season. Every hunter can improve his skills, by using Zumbo's proven techniques -- no matter WHEN he or she hunts. This book is jammed with tips, techniques, and photos. Softcover. 200 pages.
ISBN 0-9624025-0-8. $14.95 plus $4.00 shipping and handling.

HUNT ELK

The most comprehensive book ever written on elk hunting. This 260 page hardcover describes everything you've ever wanted to know about elk - bugling, hunting in timber, late season hunting, trophy hunting, solid advice on hunting on your own or with an outfitter, and lots more.
ISBN 0-83290383-3. $24.95 plus $4.00 shipping and handling.

JIM ZUMBO'S HOT OUTFITTERS LIST

The information you've always wanted! Includes names, addresses, phone numbers, description of outfitter's territory, operation, and details of Zumbo's actual hunts. 47 Outfitters listed. Plus -- What you absolutely must know before hiring an outfitter, examples of nightmare hunts, how to make the best of your guide, how to plan your hunt, and western big game information. Booklet, 14 pages. $9.95 plus $4.00 shipping and handling.

Other Products By Jim Zumbo

E-Z COW CALL

The most versatile, easy-to-use call ever invented. Attracts elk before, during, and after the bugling season. Stops spooked elk. Reassures wary elk. Also calls and stops deer, bear and coyotes. Made of soft pliable plastic and is easy to blow. Both calling edges are of different lengths to allow calls of varying pitches. $9.95 plus $4.00 shipping and handling.

E-Z COW CALL
INSTRUCTIONAL AUDIO TAPE CASSETTE

You can be a successful elk hunter. Jim Zumbo's 30-minute audio-cassette tape will reveal how and why the E-Z COW Call works on bulls and cows, reassures alarmed elk, calls elk all season long, and more. Elk are vocal year-round, and you can imitate the "chirp" made by cows, calves, and bulls. Jim Zumbo's instructional tape details when and how to use his E-Z Cow Call, a versatile tool that belongs in every elk hunter's pocket. $9.95 plus $4.00 shipping and handling.

ORDER TODAY
CALL 1-800-673-4868, (307) 587-5486

OR SEND YOUR REQUEST AND PAYMENT TO
WAPITI VALLEY PUBLISHING COMPANY
P.O. Box 2390, Cody, WY 82414